IN FOCUS

HAITI

A Guide to the People, Politics and Culture

Charles Arthur

LATIN AMERICA BUREAU

INTERLINK BOOKS
NEW YORK

This edition first published in 2005 by

Interlink Books
An imprint of Interlink Publishing Group, Inc.
46 Crosby Street, Northampton, Massachusetts 01060
www.interlinkbooks.com

Library of Congress Cataloging-in-Publication Data

Arthur, Charles, 1960-
  Haiti in focus : a guide to the people, politics & culture / Charles
Arthur.
      p. cm.
Includes bibliographical references.
  ISBN 1-56656-359-3
  1. Haiti--Guidebooks. 2. Haiti--History. I. Title.
F1915.5 .A78 2001
917.29404'73--dc21

                                    2001004426

Editing: Jean McNeil
Cover photograph: Leah Gordon
Cover design: Andy Dark
Design: Liz Morrell
Cartography and diagrams: Catherine Pyke

Already published in the *In Focus* series:
Belize, Brazil, Chile, Costa Rica, Cuba, Dominican Republic, Eastern
Caribbean, Ecuador, Guatemala, Jamaica, Mexico, Nicaragua, Peru

Printed and bound in Korea

CONTENTS

INTRODUCTION

Where, according to Condé Nast *Traveler* magazine, is the best beach in the Caribbean? In which country can you find one of the oldest and best-preserved French forts in the New World? Where were Fugees rap stars, Wyclef Jean and Praz Michel, born? Which was the first Caribbean national team to ever qualify for soccer's World Cup finals? Artisans from which country produce nearly all the crafts sold to tourists in the Caribbean region? Where can you find the world's smallest bird? In which country did factory workers once produce all the baseballs for the US leagues? Which country is currently the second largest exporter of mangoes in the Americas?

The answer to these questions is one surely that few people would guess: the Republic of Haiti. Most everyone has some idea of Haiti – it's the poverty-stricken country where "Voodoo" is practiced, and from where the "boat people" fled to escape the terror of Duvalier's Tontons Macoutes. While mention of other Caribbean nations summons up images of holidays on sun-kissed beaches, of rum and rhythms under the palm trees, Haiti almost always evokes negative associations. The genesis of this bad press can be traced back to the slave uprising and revolution 200 years ago. Then, the world's first black republic was made an international pariah by the great powers who feared the Haitian example would threaten their slave-based empires. Racist stereotyping of Haiti and its people deepened during the nineteen years of US occupation in the early twentieth century. In more recent times, novels such as Graham Greene's *The Comedians*, and films like the James Bond caper, *Live and Let Die*, and Wes Craven's horror flick, *The Serpent and the Rainbow*, have made the "nightmare republic" a part of popular consciousness in North America and Europe.

Haiti is indeed a society quite distinct from those found in the rest of the region, but the cliches of black magic and thugs in sunglasses barely touch on the reality of life for those who make up the third largest population in the Caribbean. Despite the United Nations military intervention in 1994, which briefly made Haiti front-page news, the country remains little known or understood. Haiti's relative inscrutability and obscurity means that in a world of increasing uniformity, it is one of the most authentic countries the intrepid traveler can visit in the western hemisphere. At the same time, the many misconceptions that shroud the country in mystery work against social development and integration into a larger global economy.

1.   LAND AND PEOPLE

"Haiti is like an accordion – sometimes it's big, sometimes it's small."
André Pierre, Haitian artist

A little smaller than the US state of Maryland and a little larger than Wales, the Republic of Haiti is a small country with a population that is growing in size at an alarming rate. In 1950, the estimated population size was just over three million people, but within a mere 30 or so years it had risen to approximately five million. By the end of the last century, the number had grown to around seven and a half million. A current population growth rate of over 2 percent a year indicates that the inhabitants of this nation could total some 10 million by 2010, and 20 million by the year 2040. With a surface area of just 10,951 miles (27,797 km^2), there are already an average of approximately 700 people for each square mile, making Haiti second only to Barbados as the most densely populated country in all the Americas. Considering the fact that parts of the vast mountain ranges that traverse the country remain completely uninhabitable, the actual population density is greater still.

Roots of the Haitian People

The original inhabitants of this land when European colonization began in the late fifteenth century were Tainos, a branch of the Arawak people who populated the northern Caribbean islands. Within a few decades, ill treatment at the hands of the Spanish colonizers and the spread of European diseases exterminated the entire Taino population. From then on, the island's population was composed of Europeans and the black Africans they imported to work as slaves. For two centuries the island remained sparsely populated, and it was not until the eighteenth century, when the French began to import large numbers of African slaves to work on newly established plantations in the western territories, that the roots of the population of what is now the Haitian nation began to form.

The defining event in early Haitian history was the revolution that overthrew this slave system. When it began in 1791, there were about half a million black slaves living in the western, French-controlled colony, then known as Saint Domingue, and of this number an estimated two-thirds had been born in Africa. According to the records of the slavers, their captives came from all across west and central Africa, from different tribes and linguistic groups. Yet within a short period of time they emerged from the experience of plantation life, and twelve years of revolutionary

Statue of the unknown slave in front of the Presidential Palace *Jean-Léo Dugaste/Panos Pictures*

upheaval, as a people linked together by a common language, and by shared history and beliefs. The vast majority of today's Haitians are descendents of these people.

At the outbreak of the revolution, the white colonists formed a population some 40,000-strong, but over the following twelve years, loss of life and emigration during the revolutionary wars, and the subsequent massacre of those remaining in the early months of independence, effectively eradicated the white presence. The only group of any significance that survived was the remnant of a force of 2,570 Polish mercenaries sent by Napoleon in the summer of 1803, who had promptly switched sides and joined the revolution. They were allowed to remain in the new black republic, and today some of their descendents are to be found in and around the village of Cazales, 30 miles north of Port-au-Prince.

Joining the black former slaves as the inheritors of the newly independent state of Haiti were the children of unions between white male owners and black female slaves. At the time of the revolution, this group, known as mulattos – a term not regarded as offensive in Haiti, either then or now – numbered around 27,000. Unlike in other slave-based colonies, many of Saint Domingue's mulattos had been recognized by their fathers, provided with an education, and even allowed to inherit property and themselves own slaves. Although by no means treated as the equals of whites, such a relatively privileged social position did not induce the mulattos to make immediate common cause with the rebellious black slaves, and it was not until 1803 that an alliance between the mulatto and black armies finally succeeded in defeating the French. Then, as now, the mulattos were a minority, but one that possessed the power and influence to play a significant role in Haiti's history and society.

Since independence in 1804, the basic composition of the Haitian population has changed little. There was an influx of runaway slaves from other nearby colonies in the 1820s, and, later that century, some priests, missionaries, and businessmen from Europe and North America began to settle. But the only really significant immigration occurred in the late nineteenth and early twentieth century, when some 15,000 people from the French Levantine territories of the Middle East arrived, and soon prospered as traders and merchants. Many of these families are now leading figures in the country's business community.

Independent but Divided

Although the 1791–1804 revolution brought an end to slavery, and made both blacks and mulattos free and theoretically equal, the racial, social, and economic divisions deriving from the colonial regime exerted strong influences on the shaping of post-independence society. Even before the revolution had culminated in independence, the black former slaves, who composed the vast majority of the population, had demonstrated their deep-seated antipathy to work on the plantations. Come independence, neither the victorious military leaders who took control of abandoned cultivated land in the name of the state, nor the free mulattos whose ownership of land pre-dated the outbreak of the revolution, could make the ex-slaves return to the plantations. This shortage of labor, combined with a lack of investment capital, spelled failure for the attempts on the part of Haiti's early leaders to regenerate the successful plantation economy of the French colonial era. In its place, a subsistence economy developed as, in ever increasing numbers, former slaves squatted on idle or abandoned plantation land, or carved new plots out of marginal land on the hillsides. When the emerging mulatto political leadership began distributing small plots of state-owned land to black soldiers in an attempt to win political support, the dismantling of the plantation system gathered steam.

In these circumstances, the minority elite – both mulatto landowners and black military officers – was obliged to look for new ways to perpetuate its wealth. They turned away from investment in agricultural production, and instead focused on the distribution and export of the produce grown by the peasant farmers, and the control of state revenue, in particular, the levying of taxes.

Within a few decades, the plantation colony of Saint Domingue was transformed into the independent, but deeply divided, nation of Haiti – divided between a rural population of smallholding peasant farmers, and an urban-based commercial and political elite. The social corollary to this economic reorientation was the development of two essentially separate social realities. On the one hand, there was the vast majority, mostly black, poor peasants, and later shanty-town dwellers, communicating in the Creole language, maintaining certain African traditions and lifestyles, and developing the rituals and ceremonies to serve the spirits of Vodou. On the other, there was a mainly mulatto, urban-based, elite minority, writing and speaking French, seeing itself as European, and professing spiritual allegiance to the Catholic Church.

The New Interior

Haiti's new economic and social order formed the backdrop to a widening division between the inhabitants of the coastal towns and those who lived in the interior. In the colonial era, the population centers and main economic activities had been largely restricted to the lowland coastal plains and Artibonite valley. The mountainous interior had remained largely uninhabited, save for scattered bands of runaway slaves known as Maroons. However, during the nineteenth and especially the twentieth century, the demand for cultivable land propelled a rapidly growing peasantry inland. Successive generations of peasants moved further into the mountains in search of fresh agricultural land, and, in contrast to the rest of the Americas where comprehensive land reform never took place, Haiti became a nation of small peasant farmers.

Today, two-thirds of the population still scratch out a living from small farm plots, most of them spread across the mountainous interior. Most homes in the countryside are still without electricity or piped water. In many respects, it is the existence of this smallholding population, living a way of life that has changed little over the last 200 years, that makes Haitian society quite distinct from those of its Caribbean and Central American neighbors.

Deforestation

The division of the interior into smallholdings, combined with an absence of any significant investment in or modernization of agricultural production, also accounts for one of the most distinctive features of the Haitian landscape – the almost complete lack of tree cover. The deforestation of Haiti began in earnest in the early nineteenth century with the export of logwood and mahogany, and accelerated when land was cleared to make way for new farms. The single greatest cause, however, has been the near total reliance on wood as a source of energy, and, in particular, on charcoal as fuel for

Farmers working on tree-stripped mountainous land

Rob Huibers/Panos Pictures

cooking. By 1923, an estimated three-quarters of tree cover was gone, and, by the early 1980s, less than four percent of Haiti's surface area was covered by forest.

A never-ending demand for charcoal, both on the part of city and country folk, coupled with the use of vast quantities of wood for the dry-cleaning of clothes in the towns, have today stripped the country almost bare. The only remaining forests of any size can be found in two national parks, La Visite to the south of the capital, and Makaya, to the west, between Les Cayes and Jérémie. Unfortunately, even national parks enjoy little protection, and the trees there are now more vulnerable still as new road construction opens up these previously inaccessible areas, making it easier to transport people in and charcoal out.

The calamitous consequences of deforestation for a population heavily dependent on agriculture are clear to anyone arriving in Haiti by air. From the airplane it is easy to see the exposed rock on denuded hillsides, particularly pronounced in the northwest peninsula, and the blue coastal waters discolored by brown slicks of eroded topsoil that has been washed down by torrential showers. Each year around 15,000 hectares (37,000 acres) of cultivatable land are lost to soil erosion, and in many areas the once-regular rainy seasons are a thing of the past. For the poorest rural people, the threat of drought and famine looms.

The "Republic of Port-au-Prince"

Although the people of the mountainous interior compose the majority of Haitians, and, in a sense, also constitute the essence of traditional Haitian society, for most visitors the first (and often bewildering) experience will be the teeming streets, broken infrastructure, and run-down buildings of the country's capital city. Port-au-Prince was made the capital of French Saint Domingue in 1749, but only began to grow in size towards the end of the nineteenth century. Its position as the country's economic and political center was not finally consolidated until the 1915–1934 US occupation. Since then it has remained the focus of both political and commercial life, consuming so much of both the country's attention and national budget (90 percent), that critics have portrayed it as a state within a state, and cynics have dubbed it, the "Republic of Port-au-Prince."

In the second half of the twentieth century, the city's population exploded – from 150,000 in 1954 to about two million in 2000 – as peasants poured in from the countryside in search of a living. This great influx of people has overwhelmed the basic infrastructure, and most inhabitants must endure poor sanitation and drainage, a decrepit water system, intermittent electricity, intense traffic congestion, and inadequate garbage collection. Unregulated house construction has engulfed the once sedate and well-ordered residential zones of the city's downtown area, and new shantytowns have grown up on any available land. According to a 1998 World Bank study, two-thirds of the population of Port-au-Prince lives in slums.

Today, the capital is a chaotic and anarchic sprawl, stretching from the coast up the mountainsides and out onto the Cul de Sac Plain. Over time slum developments have spilled out of the city center onto the coastal flats – to the south, the never-ending suburb of Carrefour, and to the north, the notoriously poor and destitute shantytown of Cité Soleil. The development of newer, much more up-market properties has been underway since the mid-1990s, and the slopes between the Delmas road and the international airport are home to huge construction sites.

High above the congestion and squalor of downtown Port-au-Prince is the mountainside suburb of Pétionville where, amid cool and clean air, the elite families of Haiti's upper class eat at French restaurants, shop at supermarkets stocked with imported goods, and generally live in a completely different world. Still further up the mountains, to Montagne Noire, La Boule, and toward Kenscoff, are the villas and surrounding gardens where this tiny elite resides in secluded luxury behind high, barbed-wire fences, patrolled by private security guards.

Haiti's Towns and Cities

Like Port-au-Prince, all the other major urban centers are located on the coast, reflecting their origins as ports during the colonial era. The French founded the northern city of Cap-Haïtien, once known as Cap-Français, in 1670. This coastal settlement quickly prospered, and during the eighteenth century enjoyed a golden period serving as the port and commercial center for the immensely productive plantations of the Plaine du Nord. From the time of the Haitian revolution, however, what was said to be the most attractive city outside France entered into a steady decline. In 1802, Henri Christophe, leader of the revolutionary black army in the north, burned the city down rather than let it fall into the hands of the approaching French forces. Although rebuilt and renamed, first Cap-Henri and then Cap-Haïtien, the city never recaptured its former glory. An earthquake in 1842 and then a hurricane in 1928 inflicted new destruction, and hastened the city's demise. Today, though it is still the most important urban center in the north, with a population of about 100,000, Cap-Haïtien is a rather quiet and relaxed town.

Other port towns enjoyed something a boom time in the nineteenth century as those with assets and capital congregated there, and grew rich from the control of agricultural exports. This trade generated great incomes for the new urban elite, and Jérémie prospered from exporting cacao, Jacmel from coffee, Gonaïves and St. Marc from cotton, and Port-de-Paix from logwood. The fortunes of these once bustling and thriving port towns, however, declined in the twentieth century as a consequence of the vagaries of international demand for the products they exported. When François Duvalier made Port-au-Prince the only official port, they entered an economic and social torpor that exists to this day. Over recent decades, only the regional administrative and commercial centers of Les Cayes in the south, Gonaïves in the center, and Cap-Haïtien in the north have seen any significant growth in population size.

The Border

Until relatively recent times the border between Haiti and the Dominican Republic remained ill defined. Neither the French colonists in the west nor the Spanish in the east had paid much attention to the lands between them, and during the colonial period an area roughly corresponding to what is now the Haitian department of the Central Plateau had remained under nominal Spanish control. Even after Haiti and the Dominican Republic became independent there was no mutually recognized border. The population of this region intermingled and moved freely up until the time of the US occupations of Haiti (1915–1934) and the Dominican Republic (1916–1924) when a border was delineated and stricter controls were imposed.

Boston district of Citié Soleil   *Marc French/Panos Pictures*

In 1937, the Dominican dictator, Trujillo, brutally asserted Dominican sovereignty over the borderlands by ordering the massacre of as many as 25,000 Haitians and dark-skinned Dominicans living in the area, and thereafter, the racist propaganda of right-wing Dominican politicians has stirred up considerable anti-Haitian sentiment. Prejudice against Haitians among many lighter-skinned Dominicans has become commonplace. Despite this hostility, large numbers of Haitians continue to cross over the approximately 170-mile (275-km) border to find work as sugar cane cutters, tobacco and coffee pickers, and construction laborers. Many have settled in the Dominican Republic, although their immigration status remains undefined, and today there are an estimated 500,000 Haitians and Dominicans of Haitian descent living in the Dominican Republic.

Haitians Today

There are also significant Haitian populations in the French Caribbean territories of Guadeloupe, Martinique, St. Martin, and Guyana, as well as in the Bahamas, and the British dependency, the Turks and Caicos Islands. Most of these people are immigrants with uncertain residency status, and in recent years the host countries have been repatriating Haitians in large numbers. These returnees bring with them their experiences of different cultures and attitudes, but the greatest influence of this type on modern-day Haitian society comes from those one million or so Haitians who live legally in North America. Not only do they bolster a failing economy with their remittances that total as much as US$600 million a year – providing essential support to tens of thousands of families – but many return to Haiti at Carnival and for summer vacations. North American – particularly African-American – fashion and music styles are increasingly evident in Port-au-Prince and other towns.

Though Haiti is still predominantly a society of peasant farmers, it is changing. The slow improvement in communications and the rapid urbanization are creating a population ever more closely linked to the global system. The sudden jump in the number of motor vehicles in the country, from 70,000 in 1994 to about 120,000 in 1999, is an example of how much Haiti has changed in just the last few years. At the turn of the last century, an estimated 43 percent of the population was under fifteen years of age. Most of them were not even born when the Duvalier dictatorship collapsed, but they will have lived with the presence of UN troops, and the flood of foreign aid workers and consultants since 1994. They will have heard the stories of the returned "boat-people" who nearly made it to Florida, and seen television images of the United States. According to the 1999 projections of the private telephone company, Haitel, within five years it will be common for young Haitians to be using mobile cell phones to communicate with each other, and they will find it hard to comprehend how their grandparents once blew through a conch shell in order to contact their neighbors.

2.   HISTORY

"For our country, for our forefathers, united let us march.
Let there be no traitors in our ranks!
Let us be masters of our soil.
United let us march
For our country, for our forefathers."

Extract from the Haitian national anthem, *La Dessalinienne*, written by Justin Lhérisson and Nicolas Geffrard in 1904.

Perhaps more than any other Caribbean nation, Haiti is a place steeped in history. In the eighteenth century, it was the richest and most productive colony in the world, and was known as France's Pearl of the Antilles. Then the slaves rose up in rebellion, and, over twelve years of epic struggle, a succession of European armies tried and failed to crush the revolution. It was the first and only successful slave revolution, and resulted in the creation of the world's first black republic. Since the momentous events of the revolution, Haiti has experienced a tortuous development notable for political instability, a US occupation, the Duvalier dictatorships, a flowering of grassroots organizations, and the bloody military coup against the continent's first elected liberation theologist leader. In recent times, Haiti has undergone the unusual experience of a US military intervention in support of a leftist political leader. Thereafter the country has been in receipt of substantial assistance for reconstruction and democratization from the international community, but as the 200th anniversary of independence approaches, Haiti is still riven by political disputes and massive economic inequality.

The Tainos

The revolution, and its fallout post-independence, had such a great influence on the way modern Haiti developed that the country's pre-revolutionary history is often overlooked. When Christopher Columbus arrived in 1492, the indigenous Tainos numbered anything between 400,000 and one million, but within 50 years, this entire population had been virtually eliminated. Their last stand was the 1519 rebellion led by the chief, Enriquillo, who together with some 500 other Tainos fled into the mountains that today are on the Dominican side of the border. For fourteen years, Enriquillo's rebels defied the Spaniard's attempts to subjugate them, but, by the time Emperor Charles V signed a peace treaty in 1533, the genocide was all but complete.

Apart from some crops they grew, such as cassava, sweet potato, and tobacco – at that time unknown in Europe – there is little else by way of a

Columbus lands on Hispaniola; an idealized interpretation byThéodore de Bry

Taino legacy. Some historians believe that Enriquillo's rebels and other smaller bands of Taino fugitives may have been joined by escaped African slaves – the first of whom were brought to Hispaniola by the Spanish in 1502. Such an interaction could have enabled the Tainos to pass on to the runaway slaves their knowledge of the medicinal properties of endemic plants, roots, and tree leaves – a knowledge that is still utilized today by Haiti's "leaf doctors" and lay practitioners.

Spanish Colonization

The Spanish colonization of what is today the Republic of Haiti got off to an inauspicious start, and within a short period of time the western sections of the island were more or less ignored. The first permanent European settlement in all the Americas was a fort named La Navidad, built in 1492 from timbers salvaged from one of Columbus' ships that ran aground off the northern coast. When Columbus returned a year later, he found the fort burned to the ground, and the 39 men he had left behind killed by the Tainos for kidnapping and raping Taino women. Archaeological investigations suggest that the site of La Navidad is Bord de Mer, near the present-day village of Limonade.

The Spanish built a new settlement further east, and extended their presence across the island in search of gold. First the Tainos, and then enslaved Africans, were put to work prospecting and extracting gold from rivers, streams, and a few mines. When it became clear that the island would not yield significant gold deposits, the colonists instead concentrated their efforts on agriculture on the fertile plains in the center of the island. Sugar cane, tobacco, and coffee were exported from the main port and urban center, the city of Santo Domingo, in the southeast. For several decades the colony was the center of Spain's New World empire, but with the discovery of gold and silver in Mexico and Peru, the importance of

Hispaniola (the Spaniard's name for the island) began to wane. Henceforth, the precious metal jackpots offered by the mainland proved a far greater draw for new immigrants from Spain than the more prosaic opportunities offered by Hispaniola's slowly developing economy based on tobacco production and cattle ranching.

With the main colonial focus concentrated on the east and south of the island, Spanish interests in the northern and western parts remained negligible. As a result, the coastline became the haunt of French and British pirates who preyed on ships plying the route between the New World colonies and Europe. During the seventeenth century, these pirates congregated in bases, first on the northern island of La Tortue, and then along the mainland coast. The small island, Ile-à-Vache, off the southwestern coast, served as a base for the famous pirate, and later, colonial governor of Jamaica, Captain Henry Morgan. In the 1660s, he sailed from Ile-à-Vache to attack the Spanish in Santo Domingo and Colombia in the name of the British King Charles II. When they weren't plundering and looting, these adventurers developed a nomadic way of life. They hunted wild boar and cattle, and smoked the meat over green wood fires on racks called *boucans*. These *boucaniers* – hence the name, "buccaneers" – eventually established more permanent settlements where they grew crops for their own consumption.

Division, Slavery, and Revolution

The western territory remained sparsely populated until France began to take an interest during the latter half of the seventeenth century, and, under the influence of agents of the French Crown, a plantation economy began to thrive on the coastal plains. In 1697, Spain ceded the western third of Hispaniola to France, thereby dividing the island into the two colonies of French Saint Domingue and Spanish Santo Domingo that today exist respectively as Haiti and the Dominican Republic. Over the course of the next 100 years, the fortunes of the two colonies were reversed. French Saint Domingue enjoyed phenomenal economic success, and a rapid increase in population, as tens of thousands of African slaves were brought in to work the plantations. By comparison, Spanish Santo Domingo was underdeveloped and underpopulated.

A staggering number of enslaved Africans were brought to French Saint Domingue over a relatively short period of time – one estimate suggests that the slave population increased from a little over 3,000 in 1690 to well over 47,000 by 1720. As larger areas of the fertile coastal plains were brought into cultivation, more and more slaves were imported. Within a few decades, the plantations began to produce vast quantities of sugar, coffee, rum, cotton, and indigo. Saint Domingue became the richest of all

France's colonies, generating more wealth than all the rest of her colonial possessions put together.

This prosperity was created by the labor of slaves who suffered brutal treatment at the hands of their owners and overseers. In turn, they responded in a variety of ways, ranging from damaging machinery and working slowly, to more overt acts such as running away from the plantations, and poisoning the plantation owners. Some Maroons, as runaway slaves were known, would live on the periphery of the port towns in semi-clandestinity, existing by stealing from plantation fields and storehouses. Others fled into the mountains where, in time, they joined together and established permanent settlements, occasionally mounting raids on white population centers. One of the most famous Maroons was Makandal, a master poisoner who tried to organize a mass slave uprising. He was betrayed, captured, and burned at the stake in 1758.

The importation of ever-greater numbers of new slaves in order to increase plantation production levels generated unparalleled riches for the French colonists and mainland merchants. It also brought together large concentrations of slaves living in a most cruel and inhumane situation, and in so doing created the conditions for rebellion and uprising. The ideals of the 1789 French Revolution encouraged Saint Domingue's mulattos to agitate for equal political rights with the whites. In August 1791, however, their rebellion was quickly overtaken when the black slaves finally rose up.

Bois Caiman

One of the seminal events in Haitian history was the secret ceremony held in woods outside the city of Cap-Français, today's Cap-Haïtien, on the night of August 14, 1791. As a violent storm crashed overhead, a gathering of slaves made a pact to exact vengeance on their white oppressors. According to legend, the ceremony was lead by Boukman, a slave who had been brought to Saint Domingue from Jamaica. He was a priest of the Vodou religion – a hybrid of the religions brought to Saint Domingue by people torn from different parts of Africa. A black pig was sacrificed and, as the assembled slaves drank its blood, they swore to launch an insurrection to overthrow slavery. Eight days later, the uprising began, and across the whole northern plain the slaves took up whatever weapons came to hand. The white plantation owners, their families, and employees were killed or forced to flee. Within months, the rebellion spread across the whole of the French colony, and so began a period of protracted warfare between black and white forces.

The connection between Vodou and the rebellion that was to eventually end in independence and liberation from slavery is the source of some dispute. Some point to contemporary accounts of the hostilities in which much is made of the leadership role of Vodou priests, and of slaves' belief that supernatural spirits protected them from injury and death during combat. Others stress the role of the bands of Maroon slaves, and highlight the value to the black armies of the

Maroon's experience of fighting the whites and their knowledge of the mountainous terrain. The doubters counsel against reliance on sensationalist accounts written from the perspective of the white slavers, and note that in fact the successful black military commanders displayed a marked antipathy to both the Maroon leaders and the practice of Vodou in the ranks. Whatever the truth, in the minds of most Haitians today, there is a strong linkage between Vodou and the success of the slave revolution. When, in the late 1990s, Protestant missionaries began holding explicitly anti-Vodou services at the presumed site of the Bois Caiman ceremony on the August 14th anniversary, there was outrage in Haiti, and eventually the authorities sent police to prevent them taking place.

How the Revolution Was Won

The slaves' rebellion developed into a revolutionary war over the course of some twelve years, as first forces loyal to the French Crown, then the Spanish, the British, and finally, the French Republicans, tried to win control of the territory. During these often-overlapping interventions both the black ex-slaves and mulatto freemen entered into a series of tactical alliances with the contending foreign powers. The commander of the black armies, Toussaint L'Ouverture, in particular, displayed an astute understanding of inter-colonial rivalries, forging and breaking these alliances to maximum effect to further the struggle for freedom from slavery.

A number of other factors also counted against the European forces. In the context of a war against elusive and mobile ex-slave armies, the Europeans' military tactics and strategy proved absolutely inappropriate. Fixed positions and static formations may have worked in Europe, but not in Saint Domingue against guerrilla forces with a far superior knowledge of the terrain on which they were fighting. The European troops were also at a significant disadvantage, being neither able to cope with the fiercely hot climate, nor with the local tropical diseases. Yellow fever and malaria are estimated to have claimed the lives of thousands of British and French troops, and the leader of Napoleon's invasion force, his brother-in-law, General Charles Leclerc, himself died of a fever on the northern island of La Tortue in November 1802.

Toussaint L'Ouverture

The man who emerged as the main leader of the black slaves' revolution was born in 1743 to slaves on the Bréda plantation near Cap Français, now Cap-Haïtien. Taught to read and write by his godfather, Toussaint rose quickly in rank among the household slaves, and became first his master's coachman, and then steward of all livestock on the estate. When the 1791 uprising took hold, Toussaint joined the bands of rebellious slaves and Maroons who commanded the north of the colony. He organized these men into an efficient fighting force, skilled at guerrilla warfare, and quickly

Toussaint L'Ouverture

won their loyalty, respect, and admiration. He soon became the undisputed leader of the black forces, making alliances first with the Spanish forces to the east, then in 1793, when France abolished slavery in its colonies, he sided with the French. Under his command, the black armies fought and defeated the Spanish, and the 20,000 British troops deployed between 1793 and their surrender in 1798. By 1801, he had become governor general of the whole island, having captured Santo Domingo, the capital of the Spanish colony, and liberated the slaves in the east.

When Napoleon Bonaparte dispatched a massive 22,000-strong invasion force to bring the colony under control of the French Republic, Toussaint was obliged to submit to these superior numbers, and on May 1, 1802, approved a truce. A few weeks later he was taken captive and sent to France, where he was imprisoned. After ten months in captivity, he was found dead in his cell of neglect and starvation, but as William Wordsworth wrote in his poem, "To Toussaint L'Ouverture," "Though fallen thyself, never to ride again, Live and take comfort. Thou has left behind Powers that will work for thee."

Jean-Jacques Dessalines

The other founding father of the independent republic of Haiti, who, like Toussaint, still has roads and schools named in his honor, was Jean-Jacques Dessalines. The history books have it that this illiterate former slave, whose back bore scars from his owner's whip, had already escaped to join the bands of runaway slaves in the forests and mountains before the revolution began. He became one of the principal officers in Toussaint's black army, and after Toussaint was taken prisoner, he took up the fight against the French. In April 1803, Dessalines met with Alexander Pétion, a leader of the mulatto forces, and the latter agreed to switch sides and make common cause with the black armies. At this meeting at the coastal town of Arcahaie, Dessalines created the Haitian flag by tearing the white band from the French tricolor, eliminating the symbol of the whites and joining the blue and the red, representing the blacks and the mulattos, together.

The combined forces of Dessalines and Pétion overcame the French troops, capturing the capital, Port-au-Prince, in October 1803 and, a month later, at Vertières, outside Cap-Français, the conclusive battle was fought. The defeated French forces left the colony, and on January 1, 1804, Dessalines read the Proclamation of Independence, swearing "to renounce France forever and to die

Dessalines

rather than live under domination." **Dessalines is remembered for his bloodthirsty, battle cry, "*Koupe tèt, boule kay*" (cut off heads, burn down houses), and for ordering the massacre of all remaining whites in the first months of independence. His strong, decisive, and often ruthless leadership is still revered by Haitian nationalists across the political spectrum.**

Independence and Dependence

Dessalines was assassinated in 1806 and was succeeded by Henri Christophe, who used military force to attempt to revive the plantation-based export system. The extent of his rule, though, was restricted to the north of the newly independent Haiti because, the following year, the mulatto-controlled southern part of the country seceded. The southern republic's leader, Pétion, began the distribution of agricultural land to individual owners. In the north, meanwhile, Christophe made himself king, gave his supporters aristocratic titles, and oversaw the construction of a massive fortress in the mountains to the south of the Cap. The Citadelle of La Ferrière was designed to ensure that an expected French invasion could be repulsed, but Christophe was overthrown not by foreigners but by his own subjects. Tired of forced labor and a military regime, they rebelled against Christophe's rule in 1820. The country was then reunited by the southern mulatto leader, Jean-Pierre Boyer, who, recognizing the impossibility of reconstructing a plantation economy, continued Pétion's distribution of state-owned land.

At one level, independent Haiti developed in isolation – often the only point of contact with the outside world for peasant farmers was with the middlemen who came to buy their crops to sell at the export houses in the ports. But on another, even though the country was subject to a political and diplomatic blockade, the European powers soon developed a powerful position in relation to Haiti's economy. As the political scientist, Michel-Rolph Trouillot, has pointed out, Haiti was in fact the earliest testing ground for neo-colonialism as British, French, Spanish, German, and US merchants and firms became well established.

In a manner that was to be repeated across the Third World over a century later on, Haiti became a creditor nation. In 1825 President Boyer agreed to pay 150 million francs in compensation for the French colonist's losses during the revolution. In return, France finally officially recognized Haiti's independence. This massive amount represented ten times the country's entire national revenue, and it was only paid by borrowing from European bankers. By the end of the nineteenth century, an estimated 80 percent of national revenue was devoted to the repayment of debts.

Boyer sent forces to occupy the former Spanish colony of Santo Domingo, and for over twenty years the Haitian government administered the whole island. But with the collapse of the Boyer regime in 1843, Dominican nationalists soon asserted their independence. The period of relative stability in Haitian politics also came to an end, and for the rest of the nineteenth century, a succession of governments were installed, then quickly overthrown. Sections of the small elite used force to win control of the state apparatus, and typically used the presidency as a means to further their individual financial interests in the shortest possible time before rivals conspired to unseat them. During this era, the minority mulatto elite exercised real political power by controlling and manipulating members of the black elite and black military officers, who were allowed to occupy only figurehead positions.

US Occupation

The US did not recognize Haitian independence until 1862 when the US Civil War created a demand for Haitian cotton in the northern states, but by the beginning of the twentieth century, private US business interests in Haiti had grown in the form of investments, particularly in the areas of tropical fruit, sugar, transportation, and banking. A small, 200-strong, German community had also developed a stranglehold over major commercial transactions in Haiti, and with the opening of the Panama Canal and the outbreak of the First World War in 1914, the US moved to secure its strategic and business interests in Haiti. Citing a breakdown in law and order following the overthrow and murder of President Sam, in 1915, a force of 2,000 US Marines invaded the country.

When the Marines began to force Haitian peasants into labor gangs to carry out public works, such as road-building, antipathy to the occupation quickly developed. In the remote central and northeastern parts of Haiti, a former Haitian army officer, Charlemagne Péralte, mobilized a force of several thousand peasant irregulars to fight against the US troops. He was betrayed, captured, and shot by the marines in 1919, and a photograph picturing the dead leader tied to an upright door became a new icon in the pantheon of Haitian nationalism. The US forces' superior numbers and firepower soon crushed the guerrilla rebellion. Although deeply unpopular with Haitians of all classes and colors, the occupation continued for nineteen years. It firmly established US hegemony, and had long-lasting effects upon the nation's socio-political development. One of its most nefarious legacies was the replacement of the existing Haitian army with a centralized

Baby Doc and his wife, Michèle, welcome Pope John Paul II in 1983

military and rural police corps, specially trained to repress internal dissent and maintain the status quo.

The Duvalier Dictatorships

Well into the twentieth century, formal politics was marked by the almost complete exclusion of the majority population. Only in the 1940s and 1950s, when radical intellectuals tried to reach out to hitherto ignored peasants, and when the first workers' unions were formed, did formal political activity move outside the officers' mess and the dining rooms of the elite. This political window was however soon firmly shut with the arrival of the François Duvalier dictatorship.

The mulatto elite had continued to hold the reins of power until François "Papa Doc" Duvalier, proposing an alliance between the new black middle class and the black masses, won election as president in 1957. Although elected with military backing, Duvalier moved swiftly to create his own armed power base in the form of a presidential militia, dubbed the "Tonton Macoutes." Employing indiscriminate violence against all opposition, whether real, potential, or imagined, Duvalier established a brutal dictatorship. All major institutions in civil society, including political parties, workers' unions, peasant cooperatives, and student associations were crushed or infiltrated, and as many as 30,000 of his opponents were killed. One who survived, described the negative effect of the straightjacket applied by the Duvalier regime, "If you had talent or ambition, and wanted to stay in Haiti, you had two alternatives: You could let yourself be totally corrupted, or you could be killed. That was it." Not surprisingly, tens of thousands of educated Haitians chose to go into exile – to North America, Europe, and Africa. Despite the brutality, Papa Doc enjoyed the support of the United States, which saw him as a valuable ally in its attempt to isolate the socialist revolution in neighboring Cuba.

Upon the death of Papa Doc in 1971, his son, Jean-Claude, continued the dictatorship. Although some members of the black middle and lower middle class prospered through their association with the dictators' power structure, the majority of the population suffered from the exploitation and corruption on which the regime was based. Like his father before him, Jean-Claude Duvalier continued to drive Haiti's economy into the ground through the appropriation of foreign aid and heavy taxation of the peasantry and urban poor.

In the mid-1980s, encouraged by the emerging liberation theology branch of the Catholic Church, an increasingly poverty-stricken population began to organize in opposition to the dictatorship. Protests and unrest fueled by food shortages spread throughout the country, and cracks began to appear in the Duvalierist ranks. The young Duvalier had alienated some of the regime's traditional supporters by shifting his power base to include businessmen who wanted to modernize the economy. As the opposition movement of Christian lay-workers, peasants, students, and workers grew in strength, both the United States and the Haitian military decided to ditch Duvalier before a revolution broke out. Without the support of these significant backers, Duvalier could not survive, and on February 7, 1986, he went into exile in France.

A Popular Movement for Change

The United States backed a military governing council intended to oversee a transition to a restricted electoral democracy that would maintain the status quo. This plan was upset by the emergence of the hitherto politically marginalized majority which, following Duvalier's departure, began to mobilize and participate in a range of activities, including marches, strikes, and land takeovers to demand justice, economic development, and a purge of Duvalierists from positions of power. Successive military governments lead by Generals Henri Namphy and Prosper Avril responded to this radical mobilization with repression, and attempts to install even the trappings of democracy failed. Elections held in November 1987 resulted in a bloodbath, with the army and resurgent Tontons Macoutes gunning down voters at the polls.

Free elections, monitored by the United Nations, were finally held in December 1990. The favored candidate of the US, Marc Bazin, a former World Bank employee, was unexpectedly defeated when the radical Catholic priest, Jean-Bertrand Aristide, belatedly joined the contest for the presidency. His campaign, which he called Lavalas – the Creole word for an avalanche or flood that would cleanse Haiti of the Duvalierist legacy – captured the imagination of the Haitian people. Promising justice, governmental accountability, and a chance for the population to participate

Night-time terror expedition by "attaches" – soldiers and civilian FRAPH supporters

Rob Huibers/Panos Pictures

in determining the nation's future, Aristide won a stunning 67% of the presidential vote. An attempted coup by Tontons Macoutes leader, Roger Lafontant, was foiled when tens of thousands of Haitians took to the streets to defend the election result.

The Coup

On September 30, 1991, less than eight months into the Aristide presidency, the Haitian military, with the backing of the elite, mounted a successful coup d'état. Army chief, Raoul Cédras, an officer that Aristide had promoted, fronted the coup, but many observers saw the Port-au-Prince police chief, Michel François, as the real decision-maker. Aristide was forced into exile, and the army and police embarked on a campaign of repression intended to dismantle the popular organizations and force the marginalized masses to retreat from Haiti's political arena. For three years, summary executions, arbitrary searches and arrests, disappearances, beatings, torture, and extortion were systematic and commonplace. An estimated 5,000 people were killed, some 400,000 were internally displaced, and tens of thousands attempted to escape the country by boat.

In July 1993, a United Nations-brokered accord between the Haitian military and President Aristide was finally signed after talks in New York. The international embargo on arms and fuel was lifted, and, in return, the military vowed to prepare the way for Aristide's return. In the months that followed, the UN continued to place its trust in the Haitian military even though a UN monitoring mission in Haiti was reporting an increase in human rights violations. An organization composed of dismissed state employees, former Tontons Macoutes, and police auxiliaries, and calling itself the Front for Haitian Advancement and Progress (FRAPH), became increasingly active in support of the military regime. FRAPH carried out random assassinations, and organized stay-at-homes to protest the UN plan. In October 1993, a few days before Aristide was due to return, the newly-appointed justice minister was shot dead in Port-au-Prince, and it became clear to all that the military had cynically used the accord to buy time (as well as fuel and arms) and did not intend to honor it.

The crisis continued as the international community – led by the United States – issued strong verbal condemnations of the coup regime, but for much of the time appeared to consider negotiations a way of gaining concessions from Aristide rather than forcing the generals from power. In Haiti, the repression – with FRAPH playing a leading role – continued, but it was not until mid-1994 that renewed, and much stricter, United Nations sanctions against the coup regime were applied, and threats of a military intervention were made. Still, the military and their elite backers held onto power, and even took advantage of the sanctions to feather their nests through the control of a thriving contraband trade. For the majority, the economic crisis caused by the sanctions was extreme, yet support for the exiled Aristide remained high. Three years on from the coup, the military regime showed no sign of being able to achieve political stability.

Intervention

Prompted by the destabilizing effect on the Caribbean region of the refugee exodus, and reassured when Aristide's representatives agreed to carry out neo-liberal economic reforms, the US and UN eventually took decisive action in September 1994. Twenty thousand US troops, acting with UN authorization, were dispatched to restore the constitutional order in Haiti. The intervention was unopposed by the Haitian military, and, within four weeks, the three main coup leaders went into exile, at which point Aristide returned to serve out the remainder of his presidency. One of his most significant acts in that short time was the abolition of the much-hated army. The existing police force was also disbanded, and replaced by a new force, trained by the United States, and monitored by a United Nations police contingent. The UN took over responsibility for security from the US in March 1995, and although the UN troop presence was progressively diminished, the last soldiers did not leave until November 1998.

Alongside the military commitment, the international community pledged a five-year package of aid amounting to over US$2.5 billion. In fits and starts, large amounts of aid were indeed disbursed, but despite this massive injection of funds during the late 1990s, any concrete, positive economic impact was hard to detect, either at the macro-economic level, or in the living standards of the rural and urban poor that make up the vast majority of the Haitian population. The role played in the development of Haiti's economic strategy by international financial institutions, such as the International Monetary Fund and the World Bank, became a source of political tension, with many Lavalas supporters claiming Aristide had been

Haitian policeman threatened with retaliation
under protection by US soldiers

Rob Huibers/Panos Pictures

forced to abandon his reforming program in favor of a structural adjustment plan that would only benefit the country's economic elite and foreign investors.

During 1995, parliamentary elections returned a majority for a Lavalas center-left coalition, and, in February 1996, a new president, René Préval, who had served as prime minister under Aristide before the coup, took office. The new Lavalas government's attempt to push ahead with the program of neo-liberal reforms demanded by the international financial institutions caused significant civil unrest, and conflict between factions within the parliament. When, in late 1996, Aristide created a new party, the Lavalas Family, and criticized the government's structural adjustment program, the divisions on the center-left deepened. In mid-1997, following disputed partial elections in which only a tiny percentage of voters participated, the prime minister resigned, prompting a major institutional and financial crisis.

The parliament was split between the social democratic Organization of People in Struggle (OPL), formerly part of the Lavalas coalition but increasingly critical of former President Aristide, and a group of MPs united by their opposition to the neo-liberal reforms. As a result, the president's nominees for prime minister were repeatedly rejected, and for a year and a half the government functioned without a leader. During this time, neither the legislative nor the electoral timetables were adhered to, and loan agreements for millions of dollars went unsigned. Early in 1999, President Préval broke the deadlock by dissolving a parliament in which most MPs had come to the end of their terms of office. Elections that should have been held to choose their replacements had not taken place because in the absence of a prime minister a new electoral council had not been appointed.

Without a sitting parliament, Préval ruled by decree. He appointed a prime minister, who quickly made a political pact with a center-right group to establish a new cabinet of ministers and a new Provisional Electoral Council (CEP). Preparations for elections to fill empty parliament seats and replace all the urban mayors and rural councils did not proceed smoothly, and it was not until May 2000 that they were finally held. Contrary to all expectations, the turnout was high – over 60 percent of registered voters. The result underscored the fact that Aristide remained by far the most popular politician in the land. According to the official results, his Lavalas Family Party won a landslide victory, with only the new right wing Protestant party, MOCHRENA, recording any other significant national support. Although largely peaceful, and well organized, the elections were marred by the losing parties' accusations of Lavalas Family fraud and intimidation. These claims were boosted when Organization of American States' election monitors charged that the CEP had used the wrong method of calculating the Senate vote percentages, thereby mistakenly giving outright victories to a significant number of Lavalas Family Senators who should have contested a second round run-off. Despite threats by the United States and the European Union that future development aid would be cut off if the results were not recalculated, the Préval government refused to back down. Run-off elections for seats in the House of Deputies went ahead but without the participation of the opposition candidates or the presence of international election observers. In August 2000, amid continuing protests from the main opposition parties and the international community, a new parliament dominated by the Lavalas Family was inaugurated.

In November 2000, despite the efforts of the Organization of American States to broker a compromise, a further round of elections for a new president and another third of the Senate went on, with all the opposition parties refusing to participate, and without international observers. The opposition claimed its call for a boycott was heeded – a charge refuted by the far from impartial electoral authorities. Official results gave Aristide the presidency with 92 percent of the votes, and left his Lavalas Family with 26 of the 27 senate seats, and all but ten of the 83 seats in the House of Deputies.

3.   SOCIETY

Bay kou bliye, pote mak sonje.
He who strikes the blow, forgets; he who bears the bruises, remembers.

A Haitian proverb

When two friends or acquaintances in Haiti meet, usually one asks, *"Ki jan ou ye?"* (How are you?), and the other, more often than not, replies, *"M'pa pi mal."* (I'm not worse). The language itself gives some idea of the daily reality for the Creole-speaking majority population. Life is hard, and can easily get harder. It is a source of constant struggle to even remain at a social level that is best described as living on the edge. As there has not been a proper census since 1982, statistics in Haiti are based on estimates, but a few of these give a sense of the precarious nature of the average Haitian's life: as many as seven out of ten adults are unemployed – or a least do not have a regular occupation; at least six out of ten cannot read and write; more than a quarter of children suffer malnutrition, nearly half of the population has no health care and more than two-thirds have no access to drinking water.

In the rural milieu, the collapse of the traditional economy of the Haitian peasantry has begun to topple its social structures as well. An example is provided by the changes at the level of peasant households. Once, the woman of the peasant household would make some cash by selling excess foodstuffs, or making and repairing clothes. Today, although the weekly trip to market is still a feature of rural women's life, it is more and more common to see markets selling rice and frozen chicken wings imported from the US, and to find Haitians wearing second-hand US t-shirts and pants. As a result of economic changes such as these, young people are leaving the countryside to try to find a living in the towns and cities, especially Port-au-Prince. Others travel abroad to the Dominican Republic or even try to enter the US illegally.

This exodus explains why some features of rural Haiti, such as the traditional cooperative mode of living revolving around the *lakou* and the *konbit*, are no longer as prevalent as they once were. The *lakou* is the compound around which a handful of houses are built so that families can pool resources and share responsibilities. *Konbit* is the Creole word for the work-gang for which neighbors would volunteer to help each other carry out major agricultural tasks that could not be accomplished alone. Even peasant organizations formed in the late twentieth century to try to build on these self-help traditions are finding it hard to maintain their momentum. In 1999, a leader of Tet Kole Ti Peyizan, one of the national peasant organizations, lamented the small number of young people remaining to work on family farms. In the absence of their rejuvenating presence, he expressed fears for the future of his organization and for the rural sector in general.

It is easy to see why young people are turning their backs on the countryside. Quite apart from the economic decline, state social services such as health and education are almost completely absent, and those schools and health centers that do exist are dilapidated, understaffed, and poorly equipped. Such is the neglect of the countryside population on the part of both the public and private sector that many rural-based families send one or more children to live with a better-off family in a town or in the capital city. According to UNICEF's latest estimate, there are as many as 300,000 of these children, known as *restaveks* in Creole. The parents hope that their children will get a chance to go to school, and later find a job. In reality, these *restaveks* are usually just made to work extremely hard as unpaid servants, and are often mistreated and abused by members of the host family. Those who escape ill treatment by running away are sometimes taken in by orphanages or homes run by non-governmental, usually Christian, organizations. If not, they join other kids living on the streets – a population, almost all in Port-au-Prince, thought to number at least 2,000 – who survive by cleaning cars, begging, petty theft, and prostitution.

Education

It's a sad fact that more than half of Haitian children do not go to school. A combination of factors explains why Haiti has the lowest level of enrollment in all the Americas. In many rural areas, there are virtually no schools; also, parents often need their children to work in the fields or look after siblings and have no choice but to keep them away. Given the chance, though, most desperately want their children to get an education as a way to escape from poverty. The problem is that the state education system is deteriorating as the number of children grows. In the mid-1990s, as the government attempted to meet the requirements of the structural adjustment program demanded by the World Bank and International Monetary Fund, state expenditure on education was cut by a half. About 90 percent of schools in Haiti are privately run, and parents must pay fees and buy uniforms for their children. As of 1999, the average cost of annual private school fees in Port-au-Prince was US$12.50, but when the cost of uniforms and textbooks is added, the total can reach as high as US$40. Although parents strive hard to raise the money for this outlay, in a country where the average annual income is about US$250, many just cannot afford it.

High school girls at lunch

Sean Sprague/Panos Pictures

The private schools can be divided into two groups. A handful of religious schools located in the main cities provide the children of the elite with a decent level of education. The vast majority must attend one of the thousands of small, unregulated, poorly equipped private schools where more often than not the teachers have had no training and are themselves barely literate – there are anecdotes of teachers who refuse to employ the Creole language in class, and even though they barely know the basics of it themselves, attempt to teach in French, a language their pupils do not understand at all. Even the World Bank – a keen advocate of the merits of private education – admitted in a 1998 report that the standard of education in these schools in Haiti is even worse than that offered in the public schools. Predictably, the national illiteracy rate remains high, and the few pupils who finish their schooling nearly all fail the baccalaureate exams required for entrance to university.

Health

A shortage of safe drinking water, inadequate sanitation, and woefully inadequate levels of nutrition are reasons enough for the poor state of Haitians' health. The dire situation is compounded by a chronic lack of spending by the state over many decades, which has left the health care system unable to cope with the demand for treatment. Private medical care caters to those who can afford to buy it, while international non-governmental organizations struggle to provide a bare level of treatment to the majority who cannot. In this context, it is easy to see why the mortality rate for children is high – thirteen percent of children die before reaching the age of five. An even more shocking statistic is that a quarter of Haitians die before they reach the age of forty. These figures perhaps more than anything else, including even the low level of access to contraception, explain why Haitians have so many children: parents figure that the more children they have, the greater the chance that some will survive long enough to help them at work. Maybe even more importantly in a country with no state provision for the elderly, they want children around to look after them in their old age.

The poor health of the population in general leaves people vulnerable to the HIV/AIDS virus that currently affects an estimated seven percent of Haitians, eleven percent in urban areas and five percent in the countryside. In the early 1980s, the US Center for Disease Control identified Haiti as a possible source of the HIV/AIDS virus. As a result, Haitians, along with heroin users, hemophiliacs, and homosexuals, were stigmatized with the label of HIV carriers. Later investigation showed that this early association between Haiti and AIDS was without basis. According to the US doctor and Haiti specialist, Paul Farmer, there are significant indications that the virus was introduced to Haiti by sex tourists from the United States. His book, *The Uses of Haiti*, cites a 1984 study that found that a large number of the early cases of HIV among Haitians involved those who had sexual contact with US tourists.

Healthcare at the Grassroots

Two health centers run by progressive Haitian grassroots organizations are trying to cope with the lack of health service in the poor areas in the south of Port-au-Prince. The Women's Clinic in Martissant was founded in 1996 by a Haitian women's organization, SOFA (Haitian Women in Solidarity) with the support of a US women's human rights organization. Earlier, the two organizations had together developed a community-based program to help women recover from the politically motivated rapes committed during the 1991–1994 coup regime years. Using this experience, they established a clinic offering primary health care for women and their children, family planning and counseling, and psychological and legal referrals, in the context of human rights education and training. Recognizing the close connection between health and poverty, SOFA has helped a women's group in the area set up a sewing shop that makes underwear, sheets, curtains, and tablecloths.

In the nearby and equally impoverished zone of Carrefour Feuilles is another women's clinic, also established in response to the lack of health care for the poor. After soldiers entered the State University Hospital in Port-au-Prince and executed several patients, in 1992 a nurse who was also a political activist, opened the clinic to serve people who had suffered torture or were in hiding because of

Clogged sewers in the commercial heart of Port-au-Prince   *Rob Huibers/Panos Pictures*

their political activities. Today, the Carrefour Feuilles Women's Clinic provides health care and advice to women and children living in one of Port-au-Prince's poorest slum areas. It currently treats more than 200 patients each day.

The Carrefour Feuilles clinic's founder stresses that poor health is a consequence of inadequate social conditions that in turn are caused by massive inequality. She maintains that "the clinic is only the minimum intervention... ideally the state must take up the real problems. We are not like some NGOs who replace the state by providing private services. We are engaged in a struggle to have people's rights to life and health recognized."

Non-Governmental Organizations

Everywhere you go in Haiti, you can see signs and painted boards advertising the work of foreign non-governmental organizations (NGOs). These NGOs, which first arrived in large numbers in the 1950s, are involved in a whole range of humanitarian relief projects, from the construction of roads, schools, and latrines, to the provision of food rations and primary health care. Other NGOs carry out development projects in tandem with Haitian organizations in order to try to address the problems of poverty and inequality at their source. Included in a huge variety of such projects are those that try to help peasant groups prevent soil erosion, and others that advise coffee growers' cooperatives on marketing and sales strategies.

The quantity and high visibility of international NGOs in Haiti – their new four-wheel drive jeeps with painted logos on the side can be spotted on every major route – prompt cynics to ask what exactly they contribute

Church of St. Andre   *Marc French /Panos Pictures*

to development in Haiti. Despite their programs and projects, all indications are that the plight of the poor majority continues to worsen. Part of the explanation is that often the NGOs' strategies are either predicated on the necessity to satisfy the policies of funders rather than on the needs of recipients, or are based on the NGOs' experiences in other developing countries and are just not appropriate in the Haitian context. Another concern that has been raised, particularly in the latter half of the 1990s when a multitude of international NGOS set up in Haiti to dispense large amounts of development aid, is the absence of a coherent and coordinated national strategy. Some suggest that without this, many of the NGOs' projects will never make a significant contribution to national development, and may in fact even hamper central and local government policies.

The Churches

The Catholic Church remains one of the country's most important institutions. Catholicism is the dominant official religion, even though most Haitians at the same time believe in Vodou. The Sunday sermons of bishops and priests still carry heavy spiritual and moral authority, although their political influence has waned. Church schools, particularly those run by religious orders, continue to provide the only decent education in the country. Apart from education, the Catholic Church has and continues to play a leading role in other social sectors such as health care, human rights, and community development.

During the nineteenth century, four Protestant groups – the Methodists, Baptists, Anglicans, and Episcopalians – were present only in small numbers, and it was not until the time of the US occupation that Protestant missions, mainly Pentecostal, significantly increased their influence. They carried out a wide variety of social works including the establishment of orphanages, clinics, and schools. Despite this, it is only in recent times, with the arrival of (mainly US-based) fundamentalist Protestant evangelical sects that large numbers of converts have been made. It is hard to tell how permanent the conversions are, and there are those who suggest that part of the attraction for poor Haitians is the Protestant evangelicals' access to large amounts of foreign funding. For example, the Seventh Day Adventists' relief organization is one of the main recipients of US government funds for the distribution of food aid. On the other hand, these deeply conservative groups were able to put together a new political coalition, MOCHRENA, which attracted significant numbers of voters in the 2000 parliamentary and local elections.

Human Rights

According to a strict definition of human rights abuses, the current situation in Haiti has improved immeasurably when compared with the nightmare that spanned almost four decades prior to the return to constitutional rule in 1994. In the past, the Tontons Macoutes, soldiers, police, rural sheriffs (section chiefs), and members of the right wing group, FRAPH, freely exercised violence, including murder, torture, and beatings, against not just those suspected of subversive political activity, but anyone with whom they argued, disagreed, or had a personal score to settle. In addition, theft and extortion of money and goods were methods commonly employed by agents of the state in order to supplement their incomes. There was no recourse through the courts, as the judicial system reflected the status quo, and existed merely to reconfirm the power that the few exercised over the many. Any judges or lawyers who attempted to impartially apply the rule of law were dealt with quickly and violently.

Since 1994, fundamental reform of the forces of law and order and the judicial system has been a priority for international aid donors and the government. The disbanding of the army by President Aristide at a stroke removed a major source of human rights abuses, but efforts to build a reliable and efficient new police force have proved immensely problematic. The US-trained force, nominally 6,500-strong but in fact considerably understaffed, is the subject of criticism from nearly every sector of Haitian society. For many Haitians, the force has proved to be weak and ineffective in the face of rising crime. At the same time, the tendency for some officers to quickly resort to violence, and a number of incidents of violent intimidation and repression, mostly carried out by new heavily armed units wearing black uniforms, body armor, and masks, have convinced others that there is worryingly little respect for accepted human rights' norms. Although more than 1,100 police officers were dismissed from the force between 1996–2000 for misconduct, there is continuing concern about abuses committed by police officers. In 1999, there were 66 reported killings of civilians by the police, twice as many as the previous year.

Among a whole host of explanations why the Haitian National Police has failed to live up to expectations are the force's small size – about 4,000 officers are stretched to provide an adequate service for a population of 8 million – and low morale as a consequence of long hours – twelve hours a day, six days a week, and a monthly salary equivalent to US$300. Another important factor impeding police operations is that the force lacks a certain legitimacy both with the public and government officials. This can be attributed in part to concerns about the US's dominant role in the training of the new force, and in part to the recruitment between 1996–1999 of several hundred former members of the Haitian Armed Forces to positions of leadership throughout the police hierarchy. Many progressive Haitians regard the force as a US creation, at best, imbued with suspect US policing values, and at worst, led by officers with close links to the Central Intelligence Agency and the US Army Special Forces. On the other hand, the resignation and dismissal of several police commanders following pro-Aristide groups' public campaign criticizing the leadership in 1998–1999, has led the country's social and economic elite, as well as many political groups, to claim that the force is being brought under the control of Jean-Bertrand Aristide and his Lavalas Family Party. They point to incidents where the police failed to intervene to stop violent acts by Aristide supporters during the election campaign in 2000 as evidence of the police's true allegiance.

Justice

The police's problems with legitimacy, leadership, and politicization have been compounded by the failure to implement a successful judicial reform. Despite a considerable outlay in terms of foreign aid – the European Union and the US allocated tens of millions of dollars for judicial reform between 1995 and 2000 – the justice system remains woefully inefficient, and, in many cases, just as corrupt and partial as it was in former times. Judges at all levels of the system, both those re-trained and those newly appointed, continue the long-established practice of allowing their judgment to be influenced by bribes, and/or by political considerations. Police officers who see criminals apprehended one day and back on the street the next, perhaps not surprisingly often react by administering their own forms of punishment. Negative public perceptions of the judicial system have been reinforced by the inability of the courts to convict human rights abusers from either the coup regime or the new police force. Only a handful of low level thugs who worked for the former military regime were convicted and sentenced, and no serving police officers were tried at all. It was not until two trials in late 2000 that there was any indication that the judicial system would or could hold those responsible for human rights abuses accountable for their actions. In September 2000, the former Port-au-Prince police commissioner and three other former policemen were found guilty of the murder of eleven unarmed people in Port-au-Prince the year before, and in November, sixteen former soldiers and their cohorts were found guilty of a 1994 massacre of residents of the Raboteau slum area of Gonaïves.

Although the conditions in the country's prisons have improved considerably in recent years thanks to a United Nations project, the failings of the judicial system have created a new set of problems. The prison population has leapt from 1,500 five years ago to 4,000 in 2000, putting a severe strain on staff and inmates in prison buildings, most of which were built during the US occupation. Furthermore, only 20 percent of the 4,000 inmates have yet faced a trial, and many are being detained for years without appearing before a judge.

The increased prison population reflects a rising crime rate. Incidents of armed robbery, car-jacking, and burglary, and shoot-outs between rival criminal gangs have profoundly shocked Haitians from all sectors who deplore what they call the "insecurity." A population previously familiar with acts theft and extortion committed by soldiers, police, and other agents of the state, appears totally disconcerted by the wave of common crime that has swept the country since 1995. Much of the crime is attributed to former Haitian soldiers, police, and FRAPH members who retained their weapons after the UN military intervention. Although the crime situation has deteriorated, visitors should note that Haiti continues to be a safer country than many of its neighbors and Port-au-Prince is statistically less dangerous than Kingston or Miami.

Deportees from the US

Over the last few years, over 1,000 ex-convict Haitians and Haitian-Americans have been deported to Haiti by the US Immigration and Naturalization Service, most of them for drug offenses. The arrival of these mostly young men is causing considerable social problems in Haiti.

Many of the deportees are the children of Haitians who left their homeland several decades ago. Consequently they often know no Creole or French, having

Deportees from the US languish in anti-gang police station, Port-au-Prince.   *Leah Gordon*

either left as children or never having lived in Haiti at all, and often have no relatives in Haiti on whom they can depend for lodging or other support. Upon arrival at the Port-au-Prince airport, they are usually taken into custody by the Haitian police who attempt to disperse them to jails across the country, pending their release into the community.

Some Haitian government officials blame these deportees for the increase in common crime that today plagues the country, and in Port-au-Prince it is commonly assumed that they are linked with the trafficking of cocaine and involved with criminal gangs that carry out shootings and car-jacks. Others say that it is too easy to make the deportees the scapegoats for the social problems caused by a deteriorating economy, the failure of the UN to disarm the right- wing groups that supported the military regime, and the use of Haiti as one of the main transshipment points for cocaine from Colombia to the US.

According to Chans Altenativ, an organization that helps these young men adapt and survive in Haiti, they have not formed criminal gangs but stick together because they have no one else from their backgrounds to take care of them. Most have no experience of Haitian life, and it is extremely hard for them to assimilate. Their fashion style of baggy trousers, baseball caps, and gold teeth make them stick out a mile in Port-au-Prince, and they face widespread rejection by their neighbors.

Cocaine

There is little to suggest that cocaine use is yet a serious social problem, although it is thought that crack-cocaine abuse is increasing among young people in the capital. The massive recent increase in cocaine-trafficking through the country, however, is blamed for many crimes and much of the corruption that is common among police and judges. The US Drug Enforcement Agency estimates that the amount of cocaine passing through Haiti increased from 46 metric tons in 1997, to 54 tons in 1998, to 67 tons in 1999. For the year 1999, the same agency estimates that 14 percent of all cocaine entering the US arrived via Haiti. Most drug shipments arrive in the country on the southern coast – just ten hours from Colombia by speedboat, and are then transported overland to the north of Haiti or into the Dominican Republic. From Haiti, the cocaine is then smuggled into the United States by light airplane, or, more often, hidden in the hulls of cargo ships bound for Miami.

Cocaine-trafficking through Haiti began in earnest in the mid-1980s when high-ranking Haitian military officers established contacts with the Colombian cartels. Within a short time, the financial rewards of helping ship cocaine through Haiti were soon acknowledged to be one of the military high command's main perks. Lt. Colonel Michel François, one of the 1991 coup leaders, is believed to have dominated the business during the coup regime years when he controlled the capital's Port Authority, and was rumored to have had an airstrip built on his ranch to facilitate drops. Today, it is widely believed that drug money has flooded the country, paying for many of the brand-new sports utility vehicles seen everywhere in the capital, and bankrolling the construction of new banks, houses, and service stations, as well as political campaigns.

The Diaspora

The Haitian diaspora numbers perhaps two million people. Tens of thousands live in neighboring Caribbean countries, about half a million reside in the Dominican Republic, and there are sizeable communities too in France and Belgium. But by far the largest and most influential group is the Haitian diaspora in North America.

Large-scale emigration to the United States and Canada began in the 1950s when upper class professionals and intellectuals left in search of a better standard of living. The flow increased when the consolidation of the Duvalier dictatorship in the late 1950s and early 1960s restricted opportunities in Haiti still further. During the 1960s and 1970s, middle and lower middle class Haitians joined the exodus, and significant expatriate communities grew up in Montreal, New York, Boston, and Chicago. A second wave of emigration has occurred since the early 1970s when the first boats carrying poor and persecuted refugees arrived on the shores of Florida. The "boat-people" phenomenon has continued as Haitians try to escape from deteriorating economic conditions and political instability by taking the risky 700 mile boat trip to the north. The US Coast Guard patrols the waters around the Bahamas in an effort to intercept these boats, and return the occupants to Haiti. In 1998, the Coast Guard repatriated 1,206 people. In 1999 the figure was only 363, but no-one knows how many make it to the US without being intercepted.

Although the disapora in North America is far from a homogenous group, it has maintained close links with the homeland. Much of the money earned by the immigrants is sent back to family members at home. The diaspora also mobilized in support of the Lavalas movement and President Jean-Bertrand Aristide, providing funds and turning out in impressive numbers to demonstrate their support for democracy during the 1991–1994 coup period. According to most commentators, members of the disapora wanted things in Haiti to improve so they could return. Hopes that this would be the case once Jean-Bertrand Aristide was restored to office with the help of US troops have not been borne out, and in the last few years, many Haitian-Americans have abandoned their dream of going home. Many have begun the process of seeking US citizenship.

4.   THE ECONOMY

"A country that can't feed its people is condemned to be the servant of others."
Ansi Vixima, Tèt Kole Ti Peyizan peasant movement.

"Economy – what economy?" is a reasonable question to ask about a country where unemployment is estimated at 70 percent, the average individual income is as little as US$250 a year, and eight out of ten people in the countryside live in a state of abject poverty. A whole host of factors have contributed to a downward economic spiral that accelerated in the late twentieth century, and shows no sign of bottoming out. Haiti is the most underdeveloped economy in the Americas, and, for the majority of the population, extremely low incomes are the norm. Any visitor arriving in Port-au-Prince, however, will immediately be struck by the seemingly ceaseless activity and immense individual energy of the people. In the countryside too, Haitians are always on the move, weeding fields, harvesting crops, fetching drinking water from streams, or driving livestock to fresh pasture. The people may be poor, but they cannot afford to be idle.

Agriculture remains the mainstay of the economy. Approximately 70 percent of the population lives in rural areas, and 65 percent of the economically active population depends directly or indirectly on the agricultural sector. Typically a small peasant farm produces maize, millet, bananas and plantains, beans, yams, and sweet potatoes. Any crop surplus to the family's needs is sold at the local market. Rice is also grown in the few areas of the country where irrigation systems have been introduced. In addition to subsistence production, Haiti's peasants have traditionally grown other crops – principally sugar, coffee, cacao, indigo, sisal, and cotton – to sell for cash, and eventually to the export market.

Agriculture in Decline

Until the 1950s, the crops grown by peasant farmers were sufficient to satisfy most of the country's food requirements, but since then the agricultural sector has experienced a deepening crisis. Agricultural output has suffered from a growing population farming a finite area of land. The result has been the division of cultivated land into smaller and smaller holdings, so that by the 1990s, Haiti's 620,000 farms had an average size of less than two acres. On these tiny plots, the soil has become progressively exhausted and less productive. This problem has been compounded by the extensive deforestation of the country which has, in turn, led to severe erosion of the fertile topsoil. As yields have declined, Haitian peasants have found themselves locked into a self-destructive cycle in which the cutting of trees for charcoal production, and the farming of land higher up the mountainsides, can stave off short term financial disaster but only create ever greater problems for the sector as a whole in the long term.

The Creole Pig

The already fragile peasant farm economy was dealt a crushing blow in the early 1980s when almost the entire national pig population was eradicated. The United States paid the Duvalier regime to carry out the extermination on the grounds that an outbreak of African Swine Fever in Haiti threatened the pork industries of North America. Whether such a drastic response was appropriate remains a moot point, but the negative effects on the Haitian economy and the environment were undeniable. Over the course of 500 years, the pigs brought to Hispaniola by European colonists had adapted well to the climate, flora, and fauna, and each peasant family could rear one or two without much trouble or expense. Once fully grown, the pigs were sold to raise cash in times of need. Following the eradication of the native pig stock, a program to repopulate with pigs imported from the US proved a miserable failure as the new pigs were not suited to the conditions found in Haiti, and were not in any case widely distributed among the poorer peasant farmers. The result was a serious decapitalization of the peasant economy, and still further pressure on the remaining tree cover. Not only did peasant farmers rely more heavily on charcoal production in order to raise cash, but there was less need for the trees that had previously been necessary to provide both shade and food for the pigs.

Traditional Exports

Agricultural production for export has also undergone a significant decline, partly because peasants have been obliged to shift to growing food crops just to fend off starvation, and partly as a consequence of changes in the international market. For example, during the Second World War and the Korean War, Haiti was a major supplier of sisal, a fiber used to make the ropes that were much in demand by the US Navy. The Dauphin sisal plantation, near the northeastern town of Fort Liberté, was for a time the largest in the world, but then the international production of nylon took off, and the need for sisal quickly evaporated.

Domestic factors have also played a part in the demise of agro-exports, nowhere more obviously than in the case of the spectacular collapse of sugar production. In 1951, Haiti produced almost 90,000 tons of sugar, but by 1977 it had become a net importer. In the absence of any investment in sugar production, growers were still using the most basic production methods, and as a result were unable to remain competitive with the more advanced sugar industries of other countries. Even so, until the mid-1980s, sugar cane was second only to coffee as Haiti's most important cash crop.

Cutting down trees can erode   *Rob Huibers/Panos Pictures*

Then, in 1986, the Haitian owners of the last three cane refineries capable of producing high-quality sugar found that there were greater profits to be made from the import and sale of foreign sugar, and consequently closed the refineries down. This brought an end to sugar exports altogether, and since then sugar cane has only been grown on a small scale. It is either processed at rudimentary cane mills to produce unrefined sugar for local consumption, or is used for the production of rum, both the high quality Barbancourt, and the rough-and-ready *kleren*.

Coffee production too has declined since as recently as 1949, when Haiti was the third largest coffee exporter in the world. The coffee export trade has always been dominated by a handful of Haitian families, who do not as a rule grow coffee themselves but instead buy the beans from middlemen who in turn buy from the peasant farmer growers. Currently, over 50 percent of the market, and virtually 100 percent of the higher quality coffee trade, is controlled by the Primex company, a consortium of the Brandt, Madsen, Dufort, and Kersaint family firms. The existence of these monopolistic cartels, and the high taxes on coffee exports traditionally levied by the government, have meant that peasant producers have had to accept low prices – a situation that has only served to discourage coffee production. The steady fall in output has been further exacerbated by poor soil quality, inadequate production techniques, the spread of diseases such as coffee bean rust, and the lack of tree cover needed to protect the coffee bush from direct sunlight. Although the total production figure for coffee fell from 27 tons in the year 1992/93 to just 13 tons in 1995/96, coffee remains the most important export crop, and is still grown by an estimated 380,000 peasant farmers.

The extent of the agricultural sector's decline is such that whereas in the 1970s it accounted for about half of the nation's gross domestic product, by the end of the century it measured about one quarter. The repercussions at the national level are manifold: for example, the central government, which has long relied on customs charges on exports, has seen its revenue slashed. At the same time, food production has failed to keep pace with population growth. Today, the country must import more than half the food that is consumed, creating a further pressure on the national balance of payments.

Fishing and Mining

Fishing supplements the diet of those peasants who live on Haiti's 1,054-mile (1,700-km) long coastline, but, like agriculture, this economic sector also faces serious problems. In the absence of the capital needed to purchase outboard motors and modern fishing boats, all fishing occurs in shallow coastal waters. Over the years, fish stocks in these waters have dwindled as fishermen have used nets with smaller and smaller mesh in an effort to make a catch. Over-fishing is not the only problem. Just as serious are the effects of the vast quantities of topsoil washed into the sea during heavy rains – the silt destroys most sea-life, including potentially fish-rich coral reefs.

The mining of mineral deposits was a significant economic activity only in the 1960s and 70s when the US-owned Reynolds company extracted bauxite from an area around the town of Miragoâne, and the Canadian subsidiary, Sedren, extracted copper from a mine north of Gonaïves. The Sedren mine closed in 1971, and Reynolds ceased its operations in Haiti in 1983 because of low world prices. Prospecting for petroleum and lignite in the 1970s proved fruitless, and although one US and two Canadian companies did find gold and copper deposits in 1997 and 1998, they decided against investing in the infrastructure necessary for profitable mining operations. Today, the most important extractive enterprises are quarrying stone and sand for use in road and building construction. According to the Haitian government Office of Mines and Energy, this sector provides employment to 3,000–4,000 people.

Tourism

It may be hard to picture it today, but in the 1950s Haiti was one of the premiere tourist destinations in the Caribbean. The tourism industry took off around the time of the 1949 anniversary of Port-au-Prince's 200 years as capital. Most of the city's major hotels were built in anticipation of visitors for these bicentennial celebrations. In 1960, an estimated 80,000 people visited, but during the early years of that decade the numbers dropped as François Duvalier brutally consolidated his dictatorship.

Despite the institutionalized violence of the Duvalier regimes, tourists returned in the late 1960s and throughout the 1970s. The hotels and clubs of Pétionville attracted the rich and famous, including stars such as Noël Coward, Irving Berlin, Mick Jagger, Roger Vadim, and Jackie Onassis. Other popular hangouts for this jet-set crowd were the downtown Hotel

A fisherman repairing nets

Marc French/Panos Pictures

Oloffson, and Habitation Leclerc, an exclusive club of private chalets spaced between swimming pools and fountains, set in extensive grounds amid the urban sprawl of Carrefour. Port-au-Prince and Cap-Haïtien were also included as stops on the itineraries of cruise ships, an increasingly popular form of tourism in the Caribbean since the 1960s. In 1979, a peak year for visitors to Haiti, over 173,000 travelers were put ashore by cruise liners, but in the early 1980s, this thriving industry was effectively wiped out by international media coverage of political violence, and the US Center for Disease Control's suggestion, which proved to be wrong, that HIV/AIDS originated in Haiti.

The Urban Economy

As either ports, or the sites of markets, Haiti's towns and cities have had important economic roles, but traditionally the great majority of the population has had little need nor incentive to visit them. Crops for export, especially coffee, were sold to the middlemen, known as *spéculateurs*, while crops destined for the domestic market were transported from the countryside to the point of sale by female intermediaries, travelling saleswomen known as Madan Saras. During the nineteenth century, urban centers were almost exclusively the domain of a small elite, the wealthy and well-to-do. It was not until the US occupation of 1915–1934, when administrative, political, and military power became more concentrated in the capital, Port-au-Prince, that a significant urban middle class began to develop. An indication of just how small that urban middle class remains today is provided by the estimate that there are only around 100,000 people in the whole of Haiti employed in what may be termed the formal economy. In other words, only 1 in every 400 Haitian adults has a job with regular wages and hours, a workplace, and the minimum benefits such as sick pay and holidays.

Ninety percent of the formal economy jobs that do exist are located in Port-au-Prince. Approximately half of them are in the public administration, where significant employers are the government ministries, particularly Education, Health, and Justice, the state-owned enterprises such as the telephone and electricity companies, the police force, and the customs and tax services. The rest of those with formal employment work in the small private sector, mainly in the assembly factories, and in banking, commerce, hotels, private schools, and transportation. Non-governmental organizations, both local and foreign, also furnish a small but significant number of employment opportunities. Since 1995, the one area of employment that has really boomed has been the provision of private security, reflecting serious concerns about increased crime.

Assembly Operations

The most significant single source of employment in the private sector since the early 1970s has been the assembly sector, concentrated almost entirely in the capital. The Jean-Claude Duvalier regime offered a low-wage and non-unionized workforce, and some 150 companies, mainly US-controlled, set up operations in and around Port-au-Prince. In a short time, 60,000 people, mostly women, were employed assembling light-industrial products such as clothing, basic electrical components, and toys that were then re-exported to United States. The Rawlings Sporting Goods factory, near the airport, once supplied all the baseballs used in the US professional leagues. In the early 1980s, however, this sector too began to decline as the US companies began to send orders to countries where better infrastructure allowed a quicker and cheaper turnaround. At the time of the 1991 military coup, the number of workers employed in the assembly sector was about 40,000, and most were laid off when nearly all factories ceased production in the years 1993–1994. After the restoration of constitutional government, the sector recovered slightly, but by 1999 the total number employed was only about half what it had been at the decade's start.

Wages for workers in the assembly sector hover around the legal minimum, and even though President Aristide in 1995 increased the minimum daily wage from 15 to 36 gourdes a day, this amount – equivalent to less than US$2 at 1999 exchange rates – is barely sufficient to cover a

US-owned baseball factory in Port-au-Prince   *Sean Sprague/Panos Pictures*

worker's daily living expenses of food, drink, clothing, rent, and transportation. In 1996–1997, an international campaign focused on the low pay and poor conditions in the Haitian "sweatshops," and attempted to embarrass contracting companies such as Walt Disney and Kmart into making improvements. The public relations machines of these mega-companies attempted to obscure the issues by claiming they abided by all local laws, and by referring to a code of conduct that workers had never heard of. Meanwhile, in the factories, the sub-contractors continued to pay minimum wages only on the fulfillment of impossibly high quotas while victimizing and laying off members of fledgling trade unions.

The Informal Sector

Despite the paucity of jobs, even the remote prospect of regular work draws an estimated 100,000 people each year from the countryside to the cities, especially Port-au-Prince. An explosion of house building in the capital in recent years has created work for construction laborers, but, for the most part, new arrivals do not find jobs in the European or North American sense. Instead, they join the estimated one million Haitians working in the so-called informal sector, a term that covers a multitude of occupations ranging from self-employed traders and artisans to casual laborers, porters, shoe-shiners, and gardeners. By far the most common activities are the buying and reselling of minute quantities of everyday goods, and the provision of basic services. Streets and markets are full of people attempting to eke out a living by selling items such as used clothing, fruit and vegetables, chewing gum, notebooks and pens, soap, toothpaste, and cigarettes. Others run roadside micro-enterprises that, for example, repair vehicles or clothes, prepare cooked meals, make furniture, manufacture cement blocks, or break rocks for use in house and road construction.

Foreign Aid

For many decades, Haiti has been in receipt of foreign aid, most of it in the form of loans from both international finance institutions – the World Bank, International Monetary Fund (IMF) and Inter-American Development Bank (IDB) – and from individual governments in North America and Western Europe. Unfortunately, the period of greatest international willingness to lend money to Haiti coincided with the dictatorial and fantastically corrupt regimes of François and Jean-Claude Duvalier. The dictators helped themselves to this money, siphoning off hundreds of millions of dollars for their own personal use, and hardly anything was ever invested in development projects to benefit the majority population. As a result, Haiti's debt rose from US$53 million in 1973 to US$366 million in 1980, yet the percentage of the population living in extreme poverty rose from 48 percent in 1976 to 81 percent in 1985. Another reason for the, at first glance, surprising failure of such large amounts of foreign aid to make any real difference in Haiti is revealed by the US Agency for International Development's boast that 84 cents of every dollar of its funding in Haiti goes back to the US in the form of salaries, supplies, consultant fees, and services.

Since the early 1980s both the World Bank and the influential US Agency for International Development (USAID) have tied their provision of aid to an economic development plan focusing on agro-exports and the assembly industry. This controversial re-orientation of the Haitian economy foresaw a move away from production of food for domestic consumption, and, in its place, the growth – backed by foreign investment – of exports, both agricultural crops and assembled goods. Haitian critics dubbed it "The American Plan," and claimed that such a development plan would only benefit the US and the small Haitian business elite, while destroying the livelihoods of Haiti's peasant farmers.

Progress on the implementation of the export-led development strategy was hampered by political instability – the succession of military governments after the fall of Duvalier in 1986 interrupted the economic reform program, and deterred foreign investment. Then, all development programs were put on hold during the 1991–1994 military regime. Over these three years, the suspension of most foreign aid, the effects of the OAS, and then UN, economic embargoes, and the social and economic dislocation caused by military and death squad repression, came together

UN soldier guards a food shipment as
it leaves the warehouse

Sean Sprague/Panos Pictures

to send an already sickly economy into the emergency ward. Haiti's Gross National Product fell by 26 percent, and international assistance was desperately needed to rebuild a shattered country.

Food Aid

The US has been donating food aid to Haiti since 1954 through a system whereby the US government purchases produce from US farmers. The so-called "food security" programs run by the USAID in Haiti fall into two broad categories: direct food aid, where the produce is delivered to the Haitian government which then sells the food, and in theory uses the money for development programs, and indirect food aid where it is given to US non-governmental organizations that distribute it to hungry Haitians.

Food aid is immensely controversial in Haiti because while, on the one hand, over one million Haitians depend on this food without which there would be widespread famine; on the other, many argue that food aid is seriously damaging the Haitian economy. One of the main complaints is that massive deliveries of US wheat drive down the prices for locally produced rice, millet, and other staples, thus discouraging Haitian farmers from growing these grains, and encouraging them to shift to export crops. Another is that the high volume of food aid distributed over such a long time has encouraged Haitians, both politicians and communities, to become dependent, and discouraged initiatives to try and find a solution to the food deficit. More damning still is the contention that these effects are quite deliberate, and fit in with the US government's use of food aid to entice and/or pressure Haitian governments to adopt export-orientated economic policies.

Structural Adjustment

In the post-coup period, the international aid donors redoubled their efforts to re-orientate the whole economy along neo-liberal lines. In August 1994, even before President Aristide was restored to office on the back of a UN-sanctioned intervention by US troops, the IMF, World Bank, IDB, and USAID proposed an aid package amounting to some US$2.5 billion over six years. In return, and in what many commentators saw as a quid pro quo for US support for Aristide's return, representatives of his government agreed to implement a strict structural adjustment program (SAP). The SAP intended to narrow the role of the state and control government spending, privatize the state-owned enterprises, maintain low wages, eliminate import tariffs, and provide incentives for export industries.

Once returned to office, President Aristide remained lukewarm about the SAP, and in late 1995 he brought in a new prime minister, Claudette Werleigh, to block the privatization process. The next government, though almost totally reliant on the aid package, at first proved more compliant, and in 1996 the parliament passed the legislation to pave the way for the SAP. Import tariffs were eliminated, and several thousand state-employees were given early retirement or dismissed, but the Préval government began to drag its feet once the OPL Prime Minister resigned in mid-1997. By late 2000, only two of nine state-owned enterprises slated for privatization had been sold, and as a result of the government's lethargy, large amounts of allocated aid were withheld and even withdrawn by impatient donors.

The controversy over the SAP in Haiti was in part to do with economic development strategy and differences over priorities, and in part connected to wider questions of economic dependence and sovereignty. For example, few would argue with the need to make the government administration more efficient, or with the desirability of getting rid of some of the corrupt state officials appointed by the Duvaliers and subsequent military regimes. There was general agreement, too, that the performance of the state-owned enterprises should improve – for example, Teleco, only provides 60,000 telephone lines to a population numbering some eight million, and EDH, the state electricity company, can barely supply more than a few hours of power each day in the cities, and nothing at all in the countryside. Some Haitian economists argued that the state administration needed not only improving but also enlarging in order to provide social services such as education and health care. There was also resistance to the privatization program on the basis that, before the coup in 1991, the Aristide government introduced reforms that had started to produce a profit at some of the state-owned enterprises. Instead of selling the enterprises to investors only motivated by profit, reform of the state sector should have been continued, thus increasing government revenue and so permitting the extension of the services.

An argument over free trade and protectionism raged after the elimination of import tariffs was carried out as part of the SAP. Peasant farmers complained that they could not compete with foreign food imports, such as the rice from the US and plantains from the Dominican Republic, that flooded the Haitian market. Thanks to much greater state and private sector investment and support for agriculture in these countries, their food exports could be sold at a cheaper price than domestically grown Haitian produce, so undercutting the local producers. Some argued that vulnerable Haitian producers needed protection, and that the removal of import tariffs damaged rather than stimulated the Haitian economy, as well as further reducing the state revenue. Proponents of free trade at the international financial institutions (IFIs) countered with the arguments that protectionism had not worked in the past – pointing to the worsening condition of the economy over several decades – and that the existence of an extensive contraband trade in any case robbed the central government of any expected revenues.

Argument over the best development strategy for Haiti continues, but little evidence exists to support the export-led development plan. Agro-exports have not brought in sufficient revenue to compensate for the increased expenditure on food imports, and as for the much touted assembly sector, although manufactured goods still constitute a significant part of the value of Haiti's total exports, the assembly sector's contribution to the economy as a whole has been negligible. Not only have the US companies been granted exemption from taxes for up to fifteen years, but they are also free to repatriate all profits. The nature of assembly operations also means that as a rule there is no significant investment in machinery, plant, or infrastructure. In the case of textile assembly, mainly T-shirts and pajamas, the trend has been to sub-contract orders to Haitian companies, meaning that the US companies make no capital investment at all. In addition, the wages paid to the assembly workers are so small as to make next to no impact on their purchasing power, let alone permit any savings. The existence of these low-wage jobs provides little stimulus for the domestic economy because the workers cannot afford to buy local products in any significant quantity.

Even by the IFIs' own criteria, the performance of the Haitian economy in recent years has failed to live up to their expectations. In 1996, the World Bank stated it hoped for an annual growth rate of

4 percent. But even if such a rate were achieved, the economy would not return to its pre-1991 coup level until the year 2002, and, in fact, the average growth rate for the period 1995/96 to 1997/98 was only 2.3 percent. All the while, as the development aid loans poured in, Haiti was continuing to run up a larger and larger foreign debt. By the year 2000, the amount due to be repaid annually had reached some US$45 million.

The Future

With the – albeit disputed – election victories of Aristide and his Lavalas Family Party in 2000, it seems unlikely that the new government will implement the IFIs' economic development strategy with any enthusiasm. (Haiti's reliance on foreign aid will however doubtless induce at least lip service agreement to continue with some of the neo-liberal reforms.) Instead, according to Aristide's recent statements, there will be renewed focus on the agricultural sector in order to increase both food and export-crop production.

In this context, a number of ideas have been proposed. One of these involves the modernization of the sugar industry, which is currently served by about 4,000 rudimentary cane mills. These mills have a syrup extraction rate of only 40 percent – only half the rate possible in modern sugar refineries. The Préval government has already invested US$2 million in the revamping of a modern but abandoned sugar refinery near the town of Léogâne, and with the assistance of Cuban technicians it is soon expected to produce over 2,000 tons of sugar each day. More aggressive marketing of Haitian rum on the international market could also stimulate sugar cane production. The Barbancourt rum company already makes annual sales of about US$6 million, and no one has yet thought to produce an organic rum – easy enough in a country where pesticides are rarely used.

Coffee production too has already received some attention from European NGOs, which have promoted fair trade arrangements that bypass the traditional monopolies to the benefit of cooperative producers. It is possible too that with some investment Haiti can revive the once lucrative but now depressed essential oils sector. A mainstay of this sector was vetiver grass which, when steam distilled, produces a red-brown aromatic oil used in the manufacture of perfume. In the 1950s and 60s, Haitian vetiver oil was considered a high quality variety, and with a current selling US price in the region of US$12 per fluid ounce it could again be profitable.

Newer export crops like avocados and mangoes have been produced with some success in recent years, and there is potential for crops such as onions, hot peppers, and other spices. With investment, more could be done to take advantage of Haiti's climate, and its proximity to the US market. At the Ministry of the Environment, bureaucrats boast about the over 150 varieties of Haitian mango, only one of which (Francis) is currently exported, and advocate the promotion of Haitian mangoes to meet a growing international appetite for this fruit.

Aristide has spoken of his wish to support cooperatives, and has used his Foundation for Democracy as a model for this form of development. According to data released by the Haitian Unibank, the cooperative movement is one of the few areas of economic development that has experienced growth in recent years. (The number of cooperatives increased from 296 in 1995 to 1,500 in 1999, at which time they involved some half a million people). Government support for rural-based cooperatives, and for peasant associations, in the form of better terms of credit, subsidized inputs, such as seed and fertilizer, and subsidized and/or improved transportation would help rural economic development in general. A far more wide-ranging and radical overhaul of the agricultural sector as a whole, however, would be needed to increase domestic food production.

Agrarian Reform

Foreign experts mostly agree with Haitian agronomists that the small size of Haitian farm plots, and the long history of neglect and exploitation, have seriously damaged the ability of peasant farmers to produce food for the domestic market. Consequently, in 2000, the United Nations Food and Agriculture Organization ranked Haiti as the world's third hungriest country (behind Somalia and Afghanistan), and estimated that 62 percent of Haitians were undernourished. Most aid donors and lenders have concluded that reviving the agricultural sector is not viable, and since the return to constitutional government in 1994, only the European Union (EU) appeared to seriously consider the future of the agricultural sector. In line with Haitian agronomists who have not given up on peasant agriculture, an EU development strategy paper acknowledged the need for a redistribution of fertile lands on the plains and in valleys in order to relieve the pressure on unsuitable land in the mountains. In the interests of reaching a consensus with the other major aid providers, the EU did not follow through with its idea, and throughout the Préval era, agrarian reform remained an idea discussed but not properly implemented. President Préval did distribute several thousand acres in small plots to peasants in the Artibonite, but much more would be needed to be done to seriously revitalize Haitian agriculture.

A meaningful agrarian reform would entail dispossessing the large landlords who have, by hook or by crook, accrued sizeable holdings of what was originally state land in the most fertile cultivated areas. Few of them actually farm this land themselves, and instead it is either left idle or leased to peasants on a share-cropping arrangement – the peasant farmer

Foreign aid funded avocado planting project   *Marc French/Panos Pictures*

pays rent in the form of a share, usually around half, of each annual harvest. Whether it is idle land that has been squatted or a share-cropped plot, the lack of secure tenure dissuades the farmers from investing in the long development of the land, such as construction of irrigation canals, or the growing of trees. Sharecroppers are of course unable to leave the land fallow. In this context, declining yields and soil exhaustion can only be addressed by a major redistribution of land, and a major investment in public works programs such as irrigation systems, road-building, and reforestation. It is hard to see where a government without support from foreign finance could find the funds to afford to implement such a program. Without a complete transformation of the country's political and economic system, it harder still to see how a government could feel politically secure enough to risk the wrath of dispossessed landowners.

Crafts and Tourism

Less controversial, but only partial, remedies for Haiti's economic malaise are the redevelopment of the craft and tourism industries. Since the 1950s, Haitian naïve painting has been collected by individuals and museums, and for several decades Haitian artisans produced high quality decorative items for sale to visitors and elsewhere in the region. By 1990, an estimated 400,000 people were engaged in craft production, such as basketry, embroidery and needlework, leather goods, pottery, metalwork, and papier maché. Most worked in family enterprises or small workshops, but others were employed in urban factories. The bulk of sales were to the low-cost tourist market in the Caribbean, but, even so, crafts accounted for 12.6 percent of national export sales in 1990 with a declared value of US$9 million. The 1991 coup and the subsequent economic and social collapse brought the craft sector to its knees, and in the absence of any real assistance from the government or from foreign aid, its potential remains unfulfilled. As with the case of small peasant farmers, in order to revive their fortunes, Haiti's artisans need access to credit at realistic rates, and support for the marketing and distribution of their products.

More attention has been paid to tourism. Like crafts, this already weak sector had been further depressed by the political turmoil that followed the 1991 military coup. The few visitors who ventured to Haiti during these years were mainly foreign correspondents or humanitarian relief agency workers. Even the one cruise ship that still called in Haiti, at the Labadie beach near Cap-Haïtien, suspended its stop in 1991. Such was the decline, that by 1994, in the whole country there were only nine hotels with about 500 beds regarded as meeting international standards. In 1996, the Haitian government published its plan to reinvigorate Haitian tourism, and emulate the recent success of neighbors Jamaica, Cuba, and the Dominican Republic. The plan had a short-term focus of attracting more visitors from the Haitian disapora, particularly from the United States, encouraging tours from the Dominican Republic, and negotiating new port stops with cruise companies.

With the resumption of the cruise ship stop at Labadie, and the reopening of the Club Med at Montrouis, there was early optimism that Haitian tourism would take off again. It soon became clear, however, that continued political instability, negative international press coverage, and a lack of significant improvements in crucial infrastructure – roads in particular – would deter any major investment. Efforts to attract cruise ships to Cap-Haïtien and Jacmel have yet to produce results, and, in 1999, Club Med closed down again, citing insufficient numbers of visitors. While in 1999, the Dominican Republic attracted some two and half million visitors, in Haiti there were only 50,000, and about 95 percent were Haitians from the disapora returning to visit their relatives. While Haiti remains politically volatile and economically underdeveloped, the development of cruise ship and Dominican-style enclave resort tourism will have to wait. In any case, in both the short and long term, it would appear that if tourism is to bring real benefits to the Haitian poor rather than just the investors, more needs to be done to promote cultural and environmental tourism.

5.   POLITICS

"Tout moun se moun."
Everybody is somebody.

Jean-Bertrand Aristide

In contrast to most other countries in the region, politics in Haiti cannot be explained by the influence of colonial ties, nor seen through the prism of Cold War rivalries, nor explained by the interplay of traditional political parties.

Perhaps the most remarkable feature of recent Haitian politics has been the emergence of a vibrant grassroots movement for political change and participatory democracy. The flourishing of this movement after the 29-year dictatorship of Duvalier father and son, the country's subsequent struggle against "Duvalierism-without-Duvalier," and its apparent victory with the election of President Jean-Bertrand Aristide in 1990, form the essential background to an understanding of the current situation.

The heyday of Haiti's grassroots popular movement was the late 1980s, when the years of patient discussion, reflection, and organizing at the local community level, both in the urban slums and the countryside fields, came to fruition. In all corners of the country there were mass mobilizations to protest against military and Duvalierist rule, demanding fundamental social and political change. This amorphous movement called for not just the overthrow of the Duvalierist system and free democratic elections, but also voiced a whole range of other demands including land reform, the creation of an impartial judiciary, rights for workers and for women, better health and education – in short, a radical break with the past, and the creation of a completely new society. The 1991 military coup was a violent reaction to the challenge to the status quo that this movement posed. The legacy of that reaction and the eventual restoration to office of the deposed Aristide continue to affect the contemporary Haitian political scene.

The *Ti Legliz:* The Little Church

Much of the unique strength and vitality as well as one of the inherent weaknesses of this radical grassroots movement lay in its origins in the Catholic Church. During most of the Duvalier era, nearly all the political leaders who opposed the dictatorship lived abroad in exile. From the time of the crushing of the Haitian Communist Party in 1968, political activity and organizing in the country was carried out almost exclusively under the protective shield of the Catholic Church. Although this was an essentially conservative body that followed the Vatican's line, and supported the status quo – not least in the interests of defending its considerable land holdings – by the late 1970s a number of factors combined to give the Church a more progressive character.

On the one hand, parts of the hierarchy had grown unhappy with the power of the Duvalier dictatorship, and desired more institutional autonomy. On the other, the base of the Church was increasingly influenced by the liberation theology that was sweeping Latin America. Across the country, priests and lay-workers put these ideas into action. For example, several religious orders, such as the Scheut Fathers, the Salesians, Mont Fortains, and the Dominicans, focused their attentions on working with the populations of the poorest, slum and rural areas. Numerous church-sponsored training centers in different parts of the country also played a significant part in educating and preparing the leadership of the grassroots organizations that flourished in the mid-1980s.

The Pope's 1983 visit to Haiti, and his comment, "Things must change," inspired the progressive elements within the Church to take more active positions with regard to social and political issues. Parish priests gathered their congregations together to discuss the causes of their suffering, and these small community groups helped to build a vibrant liberation theology movement known as the *ti legliz*, the little church, to distinguish it from the formal Church hierarchy. Inspired by the Creole-language broadcasts of the Bishops' Radio Soleil station, this movement was a major catalyst in the uprisings that forced Jean-Claude Duvalier to leave the country in 1986. At that stage the hierarchy, which up until then had condoned the *ti legliz* movement, became alarmed by the increasing radicalization of the population in general and of some Catholic priests in particular. By replacing the progressive staff at Radio Soleil, and abandoning the prominent Misyon Alfa literacy program in 1987, the hierarchy signalled its belief that the movement for change in Haiti had gone far enough.

From then on, the split between the hierarchy and the *ti legliz* grew into a chasm. The hierarchy tried but failed to rein in the more radical priests. When the Salesian priest Father Jean-Bertrand Aristide was elected President in 1990, the archbishop of Port-au-Prince seemed to invite a coup d'état when he warned that Aristide would establish a "socialist-Bolshevik regime." Only one of Haiti's nine bishops, Willy Romélus of Jérémie, continued to back the popular movement for human rights, justice and democracy. Relations between the two branches of the Church reached their lowest ebb in 1992, when the Vatican became the only state in the world to recognize the illegal military regime.

With the hierarchy's *volte-face* the progressive priests who played important leadership roles in the popular movement lost a certain protection from the attentions of the military and their agents. The movement as a whole also lost some of its dynamism and legitimacy as the Church hierarchy withdrew its institutional, political, and moral support. Although the restoration of the constitutional government and Jean-Bertrand Aristide's decision to give up his priestly duties in 1994 enabled the process of reconciliation between the conservatives and progressives to begin, neither the hierarchy nor the *ti legliz* have been able to fully recover. The hierarchy has lost credibility and the respect of the people, while the *ti legliz* has lost much of its sense of purpose. Progressive Catholic priests, who were formerly united in their support for democracy and political change, reacted to the split in the Church and to the new political conjuncture from 1994 in a number of different ways. Some withdrew from more overt political work, some have redoubled their efforts to support genuine independent initiatives at the grassroots level, while others opted to support the social democratic party, the OPL, that formed a new government in 1996.

Popular Grassroots Organizations

With the collapse of the Duvalier dictatorship in 1986, thousands of peoples', or popular, organizations came out into the open. In the countryside, peasant organizers helped farmers to form self-help associations. Some of these peasant groups involved themselves in local projects such as the construction of pig-breeding units and grain storage silos, while others had loftier ambitions and began setting up regional networks, and even occupied and redistributed idle farming land. In time, some of the smaller groups folded, though only to be replaced by others, and today there are hundreds, if not thousands, of small peasant groups spread all over the country. A number of the larger peasant organizations established in the 1980s are still active, including the United Peasant Movement of the Artibonite, the Milot Peasant Movement, Heads Together Small Peasants of Haiti, and the Papaye Peasant Movement.

In the urban slums, too, the late 1980s saw a proliferation of grassroots organizations. Most poor neighborhoods formed committees to organize street cleaning, to provide security and to alert residents to the presence of soldiers or police. Some of these neighborhood committees began to carry out small-scale community projects such as the provision of literacy classes or road construction. Students, young people, workers, and women also quickly put together their own organizations to press their demands. For example, on April 3, 1986, a hitherto unprecedented event took place when some fifteen different groups organized a demonstration of more than 30,000 women in Port-au-Prince. The peaceful protest called for an end to poverty and sexual violence, and for jobs, loans, and education for women.

These popular organizations brought the poor majority onto the national political stage for the first time since the early decades of independence.

But although Duvalier had fled, his powerful supporters and repressive apparatus remained, and in the late 1980s the military and Tontons Macoutes used brutal violence to protect the established order. Lacking clear leadership and any sort of national structure, the popular organizations were incapable of pressing forward with the revolutionary demand for wholesale changes in the economic and political system. Efforts to unite the organizations into a viable political movement proved unsuccessful as differences over priorities, and disagreements over the correct strategy and tactics were exacerbated by the return from exile of political leaders who were out of touch with grassroots politics. One of the main contested issues was the question of elections, which some saw as a step in the right direction. Others believed that, without a fundamental reorganization of the whole of Haitian society, elections would be a diversion that would confuse and mislead the people.

When, in 1990, the outspoken Catholic priest Jean-Bertrand Aristide was persuaded to abandon his rejection of the electoral path, and stand as presidential candidate for a coalition of small center-left parties and popular organizations, the political landscape in Haiti was transformed. The repercussions of Aristide's candidacy and landslide victory at the head of the Lavalas movement for justice, transparency, and popular participation, continue to be felt to this day.

Organized Peasants

Two of Haiti's main peasant organizations are the Mouvman Peyizan Papay, MPP (the Papaye Peasant Movement) and Tèt Kole Ti Peyizan Ayisyen (Heads Together Small Peasants of Haiti). Both have their origins in the organizing and mobilizing work of the progressive arm of the Catholic Church, and both started out in remote rural communities and later extended their activities and membership to other parts of the country.

The MPP was started up in the countryside around the Central Plateau town of Hinche by peasant organizers who had trained at the Catholic Emmaus Center. Based on a small unit of ten to fifteen peasant farmers called a *gwoupman*, during the late 1970s and early 1980s the MPP grew from just a handful of *gwoupman* to include organized peasants from across the Central Plateau department. The movement's stated objective is to organize poor peasants not just so that they can work farm land more efficiently but also so that they can construct a society where all citizens can live in good conditions. By 1991, the MPP had 2,500 *gwoupman* with 25,250 members. During the 1991–1994 coup regime, the MPP was the target of fierce repression directed by a notoriously brutal military officer, the self-styled Commander Z. The organization's headquarters at Papaye were destroyed, many of its members were killed, and others were beaten and tortured. The MPP has since rebuilt its organization and forged links with peasant groups in other parts of the country. With the help of funds channeled to it by foreign non-governmental organizations, it has launched a variety of development projects

A family in the Artibonite region
with their rice spread out to dry

Marc French/Panos Pictures

such as a lending bank, community shops, tree nurseries, and a bicycle cooperative.

Tèt Kole grew out of the peasant organizing carried out by Catholic priests and others in the barren, drought-stricken northwest in the mid-1980s. In 1987, local landowners reacted to its campaign to mobilize the region's peasants in opposition to unfair taxation by ordering a massacre that claimed the lives over 119 peasants in the small town of Jean Rabel. Tèt Kole, though, survived and developed into a national movement with members in eight of the country's nine departments. Although like the MPP it carries out development projects to benefit its members, Tèt Kole does not solicit foreign aid, and maintains that its main objective is to be part of a movement to create a state that will respond to the peasants' needs. It sees a genuine and meaningful grassroots democracy as the way to achieve this, and in a further contrast to the MPP has remained independent of party politics. The MPP, under the leadership of Chavannes Jean-Baptiste, first developed political ties with Jean-Bertrand Aristide and the Lavalas organization, and later allied closely with the social democratic party, the OPL.

Aristide

It is hard to credit the strength of emotion that Jean-Bertrand Aristide elicited and continues to provoke in Haiti. He first gained popularity among the nation's poor when his sermons and speeches urging the people to liberate themselves from poverty, apathy and squalor were broadcast on radio in the late 1980s. He denounced the Catholic Church hierarchy, the minority elite and the US Embassy for standing in the way of the radical change that the Haitian people needed if they were to move from, as he put it, "misery to poverty with dignity." Unused to such attacks, his targets among the country's political and economic elite perceived Aristide as at best a rabble-rouser, and at worst an uncontrollable and dangerous figure who could foment a bloody uprising in a repeat of 1791.

Aristide was born in 1953 in Port Salut in the southwest, but spent much of his childhood in the poor quarters of Port-au-Prince. He was educated by the Salesian order and ordained a priest in 1982. After some years studying in Canada he returned to Haiti in 1985, and was appointed priest of the St. John Bosco parish in La Saline. There he immersed himself in the application of liberation theology, preaching that spiritual fulfilment is obtained through social and political freedom, and working with the *ti legliz* communities. He escaped numerous assassination attempts, including a 1988 attack on his church that left members of his congregation dead and the church itself burned down. His undoubted charisma, his great ability to communicate with ordinary people, and his refusal to be intimidated by the forces of reaction made him immensely popular with previously marginalized and disenfranchised Haitians. With his election as President in 1990, he became the symbol of hope for a better life for the country's poor majority. By contrast, for the country's small elite Aristide's promises to redistribute land, to increase the minimum wage, to enforce the payment of taxes, to stop drug-trafficking and to separate the police force from the military made him a feared and detested enemy.

The election of Aristide was, in retrospect, the finest hour for Haiti's popular democratic movement. Once Aristide was in the National Palace, a certain complacency set in as many appeared to view the election of a Lavalas president as an end rather than a beginning. Within a few months confusing and demoralizing disputes broke out in the Parliament between Aristide's close associates and parliamentarians elected on Aristide's coattails. When the military launched its brutal coup d'état with the support of the country's elite, the popular movement was ill-prepared to resist it. The popular organizations were the clear target of the military regime and, over three years, fierce repression claimed the lives of thousands of organizers, activists, and leaders. Organizational structures and networks collapsed as tens of thousands of activists fled the country by boat or left their homes to go into hiding in different areas of the country. By the time the military regime was removed from power by the United Nations intervention in September 1994, the popular movement was in disarray and many organizations had effectively been decapitated. Not only had many leaders been murdered, but some 2,000 grassroots activists had been granted political asylum in the US and other countries, and hardly any of them returned.

Other factors too militated against a resurgence of grassroots organizing. The general population was extremely weary after three years of military repression, and the immense economic hardship brought about by the international trade embargoes. Furthermore, as in 1991, there seemed to be a widespread belief among his supporters that Aristide would be able to do what was necessary, with the added advantage that now he had support from the United States with all its military and economic might. The more militant grassroots activists, who wanted to resume the organizing and actions that had to be suspended during the coup years, were deterred by the continuing presence in many communities of armed supporters of the deposed regime. These problems were compounded by the confusion caused by the approach adopted by Aristide upon his return to Haiti.

The Exile Effect

Aristide spent most of his three years in exile in Washington DC, where he concentrated on winning the diplomatic support of the Clinton administration. The unspoken deal he made with the US administration in return for military intervention obliged him to follow a completely different tack to that employed before the coup. Aristide appeared to accept that aid for reconstruction was contingent on the application of a neo-liberal economic plan drawn up by the International Monetary Fund, the World Bank, and the main bilateral donors. On his return, he repeatedly asked his supporters to adhere to his mantra, "No to violence, no to vengeance, yes to reconciliation." Previously fervently anti-imperialist, clearly opposed to US economic plans for Haiti and scornful of accommodation with the Duvalierists, Aristide was barely recognizable as he lauded the US for its support for democracy, headed a government committed to a harsh structural adjustment program, and publicly stressed the need for reconciliation with the Macoutes and the minority economic elite.

Aristide's role in the new political conjuncture did nothing to inspire a rejuvenation of the popular movement. The absence of tangible improvements in the economic situation and the failure to punish human rights abusers in the courts cast a pall over Aristide's remaining sixteen months in office. Although he did make one decisive move that broke the mold of Haitian politics when he abolished the Haitian army in 1995, his reputation as the savior of Haiti's poor masses became somewhat tarnished. It's likely that it would have suffered further if, as his supporters demanded, he had continued as president for three more years to make up for those spent in exile. The United States, however, insisted he step down and adhere to the Constitution that barred presidents from seeking a second consecutive term.

Post-1994, some grassroots organizations continued to make their presence felt by organizing protests against the continuing high cost of living, and the failure of both the interim and new police forces and UN troops to provide adequate security against the criminal activities of former

Aristide after laying a wreath commemorating
the victims of the military regime, 1994

Rob Huibers/Panos Pictures

soldiers and FRAPH members. Noteworthy too were the efforts of a small group to help unionize workers in the garment assembly factories in Port-au-Prince, and then in the northern orange tree plantations where oranges are grown and processed to produce an extract used in the famous Grand Marnier and Cointreau liqueurs. In such an unpropitious climate, however, grassroots political activity was on the whole limited to spontaneous and short-lived responses to local issues such as the authorities' failure to repair a stretch of road. Occasional violent protests involving burning tires to block roads and smashing windshields of parked cars have, from time to time, been mounted by groups linked to Jean-Bertrand Aristide, but although the latter style themselves popular organizations they are believed to be unemployed youths hired to flex political muscle rather than dedicated political agitators.

The Political Parties

Ever since the fall of the Duvalier dictatorship, the international community has encouraged political attention to focus on elections and party politics. Numerous elections have been held, and many political parties have been created, but, with the very large exception of Jean-Bertrand Aristide, few politicians provoke enthusiasm in Haiti, and despite much effort and expenditure no party has been able to establish anything approaching a mass membership or a national party machine. Indeed, many of Haiti's political parties are one-man bands created to serve the personal interests and ambitions of a wealthy individual. A popular saying describes these parties in the following way, "None of them can gather ten people under a lamp-post."

At the time of 1990 elections, a few returned exiles had set themselves up as party leaders but none of them elicited much interest from the public. Former World Bank employee Marc Bazin received US support and funding for his Movement to Institute Democracy (MIDH) and it looked as though this would be enough to win him an election with a low rate of participation. In the event, the MIDH's chances were torpedoed when Aristide became the candidate of the center-left coalition, the National Front for Change and Democracy (FNCD), and the electorate became suddenly enthusiastic. Aristide's victory, though, turned out to be all about the individual and little to do with the FNCD party. Again in 1995, when elections were held for a new Parliament and for mayors to administer the 133 communes, none of the myriad small political parties could offer a serious challenge to the Aristide-endorsed, three-party coalition, the Lavalas Political Platform (PPL). Right-wing and centrist parties abstained or withdrew rather than face electoral annihilation, and the Aristide "effect" ensured a PPL landslide victory.

The main party in the PPL coalition was the Lavalas Political Organization (OPL), lead by former Communist, now a social democrat, Gérard Pierre-Charles. The OPL dominated the parliament elected in 1995, and took most of the key posts in the new government of President René Préval. But soon serious divisions arose between allies formerly united around Aristide and the concept of change and renewal known as Lavalas. The OPL accused Aristide of manipulating key individuals and institutions in order to derail government policy. For their part, those close to Aristide claimed that the OPL's policies only served the interests of the middle class, the elite, and the international community. In many ways the emergence of these divisions was inevitable given that unity had been created only in response to the adversity of the coup years. Everyone could agree on support for democracy – in practice this meant backing the deposed president and supporting him once returned – but when the business of governing the country began, personal and ideological differences quickly emerged.

During the three years of political deadlock that followed the withdrawal of the OPL from the government, efforts were made to build a new anti-Aristide coalition. Although foreign organizations supported these attempts – in 1998, the International Republican Institute managed to briefly unite 26 parties – by the time general elections were finally held in May 2000, only three small coalitions, each containing a handful of small parties,

Two styles of architecture, the vernacular and the colonial

Wooden house on
stilts and *tap-tap* taxi
Jean-Léo Dugast/Panos Pictures

Hotel Oloffson, Port-au-Prince

Leah Gordon

Carnival mask, Jacmel
Leah Gordon

The vibrant visual and musical art of Haiti

Vodou flag making
Leah Gordon

JohnSylvestre and metalwork creations
Leah Gordon

Pro-Aristide mural after the 1994 US invasion
Leah Gordon

Foula, street *rara* band from Port-au-Prince
Leah Gordon

Street dancers during *rara* season, Miragoâne

Leah Gordon

had formed. These coalitions – two composed of neo-Duvalierist parties and the other of social democrats – joined a score of other small parties in challenging the Lavalas Family for control of parliament, the urban councils, and rural assemblies. Their abject failure in the first round elections on May 21 inspired an unprecedented display of unity as some fifteen of the main opposition parties immediately formed a coalition.

The Democratic Convergence brought together an incongruous line-up of social democrats, right-wing Protestants, and neo-Duvalierists, linked only by their opposition to Aristide and the Lavalas Family. Their strategy, which appeared to enjoy the support of important foreign backers such as elements within the US Republican Party, was to deny Aristide and his party legitimacy by refusing to contest subsequent elections, including the Presidential election in November 2000. Characterizing Aristide as a dictator trying to eradicate all opposition, the Convergence demanded that completely new elections be organized by a consensus electoral council and under close international scrutiny. Although the Convergence's support for the revival of the Haitian Army did little to endear it to the Haitian public, it stubbornly refused to accept Aristide's offers of a compromise solution, and a stalemate endured for over a year. By mid-2001, it appeared as though the suspension of important international aid allocations pending a political accord between the two sides would force the Lavalas Family to capitulate and agree to new elections.

The Lavalas Family

Even allowing for some fraud during the vote counting, it is clear that the May 2001 general elections were a huge victory for the Lavalas Family Party, and as such proved the continuing popularity of Jean-Bertrand Aristide. This success also owed much to the mobilizing efforts of young party activists across the country, and to the fact that, in contrast to the other parties, the Lavalas Family actually offered a coherent political program. While its opponents offered little more than their virulent hatred of Aristide, the Lavalas Family promised to improve infrastructure, health, and education throughout the country, promote national production, especially agriculture, by strengthening micro-credit financing and cooperatives, and to institute reforms to combat crime and extend the capabilities of the police service.

How far the Lavalas Family will be able to go, and indeed is willing to go, in order to implement this program remains unclear. With as much as 60 percent of the government's revenue dependent on foreign aid, it is clear that there is little room to maneuver, and it seems unlikely based on past policy that the international financial institutions will bankroll an economic development plan focusing on agriculture and education. While the party retains the support of many of the peasants and urban poor who originally formed the core of the Lavalas movement, large numbers of former supporters with education, expertise, and experience of administration and planning have deserted Aristide and renounced his new party. In response to this hemmoraging of support among reform-minded intellectuals, and in an apparent attempt to curry favor with critical foreign powers, Aristide has reached out to former opponents. The government formed following his election as president for a second time in 2001 was remarkable not only for the appointment as minister of commerce of Stanley Théard, a post he once held under Jean-Claude Duvalier, but also for the appointment of the military coup regime's prime minister, Marc Bazin, as minister of planning and external cooperation.

International Relations

Since the 1994 military intervention by US troops acting with United Nations authorization, Haiti has had an international profile disproportionate to its power and influence. In the United States, the Democratic Party portrayed the intervention as a foreign policy triumph for the Clinton Administration, and thereafter Haiti became something of a political football. The Democrats sought to smooth over the cracks as democracy appeared to falter during the Préval presidency, and the Republicans attempted to hype up the connection between the White House and Aristide – the "dictator." By the end of President Clinton's second term, US-Haitian relations had reached a low ebb, with the US ending its five-year police support and judicial reform programs, and suspending direct aid to Haiti's central government pending moves to curb the transshipment of cocaine and a resolution of the dispute over the May 2000 elections. Upon his re-election in November 2000, Aristide attempted to repair broken bridges by agreeing an eight-point accord with President Clinton's special envoy. This accord addressed many of the US's main concerns and was welcomed by the incoming Republican secretary of state, Colin Powell, but US-Haitian relations remained lukewarm.

The United Nations has had extensive involvement with Haiti since 1994, with military and civilian missions present in Haiti in various guises up until February 2001. From the UN point of view this extended bout of peace-building, while a useful experience, can hardly be regarded as a success. When Secretary-General Kofi Annan announced the total withdrawal of the UN mission he concluded that it was no longer able to function in a "climate of political turmoil." From the Haitian point of view, the UN presence was at first warmly welcomed following the three-year coup regime, but then popular sentiment turned to disappointment and indifference as the realization that things would not really change began to dawn. In a startlingly candid interview with a local radio station, the UN envoy, Lakdar Brahimi, explained that the UN was present in Haiti to unsure that the majority enjoyed political power but that it would not countenance attempts to shift economic power away from the minority.

On the diplomatic front, Haitian affairs at the United Nations have been "looked after" by the so-called "Friends of Haiti" – the United States, Canada, Venezuela, France, and more recently, Argentina and Chile. In recent years there have been efforts to sub-contract Haiti`s dealings with the international community to the US-dominated hemispheric body, the Organization of American States. France, which has long rivalled the United States for influence in its former colony, has responded by driving an increased European Union interest in Haiti. The ambassadors of France, Germany, and Spain in Haiti have all been increasingly vocal in their comments to the local media, perhaps reflecting the European Union's desire to assert its influence in Haiti and the Caribbean region as a whole.

Relations with the neighboring Dominican Republic continue to founder over the issue of treatment of Haitian immigrants. Despite the stated intentions of both Presidents Préval and Méjia Hypolite to improve relations, and the European Union plans to develop the border region, the round-up and forced repatriation of thousands of Haitians by the Dominican army in 1999 and 2000 generated renewed tension.

The other countries with which Haiti has significant bilateral relations are Taiwan and Cuba. Taiwan donates funds for agricultural development projects and other government expenses in an attempt to win another friend in its continuing struggle for international recognition. Cuba, with whom diplomatic relations were renewed by Aristide in 1996 after a break of over 30 years following the Cuban Revolution, has made some high-profile contributions, such as sending hundreds of Cuban doctors to administer treatment in rural areas of Haiti, dispatching technicians to help with projects such as fresh water fisheries and the revitalization of the moribund sugar cane industry, and providing scholarships for Haitian students to study in Cuba.

The Future

Haiti's political future is almost certain to be volatile. While 85 percent of Haiti's population lives in absolute poverty, one half of one percent lives in opulence, controlling 45 percent of the national revenue. Unless both politicians in Haiti and influential foreign funders and "friends" take bold and daring steps to narrow the immense gap between the "haves" and the "have-nots," continuing political upheaval and social strife are inevitable.

6.   CULTURE

"We have stumbled, but have not fallen. We are ill-favored, but we still endure. Every once in a while, we must scream this as far as the wind can carry our voices: We are ugly, but we are here! And here to stay."

Edwidge Danticat

Over the course of nearly two centuries since independence, a distinct and unique Haitian culture has developed. While the French-speaking elite in the coastal towns has looked to Europe and later the US for role models, peasant farmers and their families in the hills and mountains have drawn on strong memories of Africa to create a way of life, a language, a religion, and forms of expression that come together in a distinct Haitian identity. Neither the efforts of Christian missionaries, nor the presence of occupying US troops in the early part of the twentieth century, succeeded in altering this identity in any fundamental respect. By the end of the twentieth century, though, outside influences were growing ever stronger. Evangelical Protestant churches can now be found throughout the country; the economy, once nearly self-sufficient, is increasingly dependent on, and integrated into, a global market, and more and more young people are growing up in urban settings, particularly Port-au-Prince, where radio and television broadcast sounds and sights unheard and unseen a generation ago.

In the countryside, popular pastimes include cock-fighting, a male-dominated activity that occupies many a Sunday afternoon; the *bamboche*, weekend community parties with drinking and dancing; and gambling on the *borlette*, the Haitian version of the lottery. Haiti remains a country where most people cannot read or write, and consequently a rich and expressive oral culture has developed. Every evening when the sun goes down, relatives and neighbors often gather around the cooking pot and the lantern to tell riddles, jokes, and stories. Both local and national news is conveyed mainly by word of mouth – a phenomenon known as *teledjol*. Two Port-au-Prince "daily" newspapers (they in fact only appear three or four times a week) and three weeklies produced in the US, all written in French, serve the literate minority. A Creole language weekly newspaper, founded in 1990 to support literacy efforts, sadly went out of business in 1998.

By far the most important source of news, ideas, and information throughout Haiti is radio. The real breakthrough in making this medium accessible to the majority population came in the early 1980s when two stations, Radio Haiti Inter, and Radio Soleil, started to broadcast in Creole, and to focus on social and political issues from the perspective of ordinary people. Other commercial radio stations followed suit, and radio soon became a potent tool in the efforts to mobilize the anti-Duvalierist movement in the late 1980s. The quality of commercial broadcasting then declined following an explosion in the number of stations during the 1991–1994 coup regime. The medium has been reinvigorated, though, by the new community radio stations established in the remote parts of the country that cannot receive FM signals from the capital. These stations, run by grassroots organizations, broadcast information about health, agricultural, and social issues, as well as relaying national and local news.

Religious Beliefs

In the opinion of a Vodou priest from the Bel Air area of Port-au-Prince, there are four religions practiced in Haiti: Freemasonry, Vodou, Catholicism, and Protestantism. His case for Freemasonry is exaggerated, and it is not in any case usually regarded as a religion. This mutual patronage network based on the European model did attract successful whites and mulattos during the later decades of the French colony, and it remained very popular with the well-to-do throughout the nineteenth century. By the mid-twentieth century, though, it was largely a ceremonial activity, and today it only retains a limited appeal with people living in provincial towns thanks to its elaborate rituals and symbolism. The real battle for spiritual allegiance in Haiti has been, and continues to be, waged by Christians against the practice of "serving the spirits," a religion better known as Vodou.

In the colonial era, slaves drew heavily on concepts and beliefs from West African religions and developed the basic tenets and practices of Vodou literally under the noses of French Catholic missionaries. The defeat of the French in 1803 and Dessalines' pogroms against remaining whites in 1804 effectively extinguished the Catholic Church. Over the next 50 or so years Vodou became firmly established as the dominant religion in Haiti. There were no regular Christian clergy in the country until 1860, when a Concordat was signed with the Vatican, and thereafter an attempted Catholic comeback was mounted by foreign, mostly French, missionaries.

An indigenous Catholic clergy only began to develop in the 1920s. It was at this time, coinciding with the continuing US occupation, that the Catholic Church launched a concerted offensive against Vodou. The so-called "anti-superstition campaigns," portraying Vodou as devil-worship, and involving the destruction of drums, ceremonial objects, and temple-houses, and the imprisoning of Vodou priests, were repeated periodically, notably in 1941 to 1942. Repression failed to turn Haitians against Vodou, and often only succeeded in forcing the faithful to be more circumspect. Ceremonies would usually take place at night, and, in towns, temples were

Vodou altar for Ezili Dantor

Leah Gordon

hidden away between the corridors and densely-packed shacks of the slum areas. Increased secrecy and a pragmatic flexibility among believers who saw no contradiction between attending a Catholic Church one day and a Vodou service the next, helped Vodou survive.

Since the 1980s, the Catholic Church in Haiti has grown more accommodating, and has abandoned its former line of outright opposition. Many progressive Catholic priests see Vodou as an important cultural element in Haitian society. The new constitution, adopted in 1987, guaranteed the freedom to practice any religion, and in 1991 President Aristide met with a delegation of Vodou priests in the National Palace. Now, however, the evangelical Protestant missionary churches, many from the US, campaign aggressively to get Haitians to reject Vodou.

Vodou

In common with other religions, Vodou has priests (male and female), believers, temples, altars, ceremonies, and an oral tradition that has enabled the essential elements of worship to be transmitted. Yet the basic elements of the religion have never been written down, nor is there any national structure or hierarchy. The essence of the religion is communication with the spirits (the *lwa*) who mediate between mortals and the all-powerful God. There are hundreds of *lwa*, who may be the protective spirits of clans or tribes from Africa, or deified ancestors, and which are grouped into families, called nations. These in turn are honored by different rituals, each with their own distinctive ceremonies, dances, rhythms, and type of offering.

The spirits are invoked during services or ceremonies that take place to mark religious holidays, to satisfy a particular spirit, or at the request of an individual or family who pay for the expenses. No ceremony completely resembles another one of its kind, for each priest/priestess (*oungan/manbo*) has his or her favorite rites and special features. Some of the congregation are initiates (*ounsi*) who dress in white, and are charged with singing and dancing. The priest/priestess directs the unfolding ceremony, beginning with a litany of saints, prayers, and hymns from the Catholic religion, the marking of the four cardinal points, and the drawing on the ground of the symbolic *vèvè*. Then the spirits are invoked, the drums roll, and the ounsi dance. If a spirit arrives, it will often "possess" a believer, briefly using their body as an instrument of self-expression. Each spirit will manifest itself in a certain way, consistent with their individual attributes. Once "awakened," the possessed person remembers nothing of the event. Drums play a central role in the ceremony, and the drummers play ancient rhythms that bring the congregation and the spirits together. The spirits will only come to dance or "ride" the bodies of the faithful in response to the "call" of the drums.

As well as serving Haitians' spiritual needs, Vodou fulfills other important social functions. Priests not only interpret the language of the spirits, and officiate at ceremonies in their temples, but also act as counselors, giving advice, and interpreting dreams and misfortunes. Many priests are also leaf-doctors with a specialized knowledge of medicinal herbs and plants. The priest is often a source of knowledge and authority in the community, and the temple and the ceremonies that take place there provide the space and the events around which communal bonds are constructed.

Vodou is also a major feature of Haitian history, culture, and identity. Haitian children learn at an early age that Vodou inspired the slave revolution that created the modern state of Haiti, and, to a lesser or greater extent, Haitians maintain a relationship with Vodou throughout their lives. As the noted anthropologist, Harold Courlander, put it, "Vodou offers doctrine, social controls, a pattern of family relations, direct communication with original forces, emotional release, dance, music, theatre, legend and folklore, motivation, alternatives to threatening dangers, individual initiatives through placation and invocation, treatment of ailments by means of herb lotions and rituals, protection of fields, fertility, and a continuing familiar relationship with the ancestors."

Artisit in Port-au-Prince   *Sean Sprague/Panos Pictures*

Artistic Expression

As Haiti is both an immensely spiritual and at the same time a largely illiterate society, it is perhaps not surprising that Haitians have a highly developed sense of imagery and the imagination. They express themselves artistically in a great variety of ways, making an otherwise poor country rich in paintings, sequin flags, wood and metal sculpture, and crafts as well as in music, dance, and folklore. Haitian art has long existed as a part of everyday life – murals decorated the walls of shops and of Vodou temples, ironwork decorated tombs in cemeteries, and elaborate sequin flags were used in Vodou ceremonies. With the establishment in the mid-1950s of the Center d'Art in Port-au-Prince by US Americans, untrained Haitian artists were encouraged to develop their talents, and the marketing of Haitian creativity began. Hector Hyppolite, a Vodou priest from Gonaïves, was one who joined the Center D'Art, and the commercial success of his canvases inspired a plethora of painters using a simple, almost child-like style, usually without the use of perspective. Their paintings have made Haiti world-famous as a source of "naïve" or primitive art.

Another artist (and soon after, a new art form) groomed by the Center d'Art was Georges Liautaud, a blacksmith from the town of Croix-des-Bouquets. He began working on decorative metal sculptures in the early 1950s, and the popularity of his work with foreign buyers inspired his neighbors to follow suit. Today, Croix-des-Bouquets is home to a score of different artists who hammer old metal oil drums into unique and striking relief sculptures. The sculptures are representations of mermaids, snakes, dragons, angels, devils, and other beasts that, for the foreigner, defy description.

In the 1980s and 1990s, the sequined flags produced in the Bel Air district of Port-au-Prince and depicting representations of Vodou spirits became the latest Haitian art form to catch on with foreign buyers. Although some artists have an outlet through the galleries of Pétionville, and through them the markets of North America, Europe and beyond, there is no structure for the promotion or marketing of art, and most rely on sales to visiting collectors and tourists.

Music

There is an immense variety of music to be heard in Haiti, ranging from traditional folk music to Creole rap singers. Drumming is one of the essential ingredients of Vodou ceremonies, and even from a young age most children are instilled with an advanced sense of rhythm. The uniquely Haitian folk music known as *rara* is thoroughly percussion driven. The basic sound is created by a group playing single-note trumpets of varying length that are fashioned from bamboo tubes, and sometimes from PVC piping. The players blow through a mouthpiece at one end while striking the side of the tube to enhance the rhythm. Other percussion, using bits of metal, glass bottles and hand claps, and sometimes the honks and squeals of conventional brass instruments, accompany and embellish a seemingly endless cyclical and rhythmic voyage. Although it can usually be heard at any event when a crowd is gathered, the main time of the year for *rara* are the weeks of Lent – between the annual Shrove Tuesday Carnival and Easter Sunday. The *rara* bands play on the move, and their infectious do-it-yourself music attracts wildly dancing crowds who follow them along country lanes and through the streets of the sprawling urban slums.

The other main type of traditional music that can be heard in Haiti is known as *twoubadou* (troubador) music. As its name suggests, this music is often played and sung by performers who wander through the streets hoping to earn a few gourdes in reward for their efforts. The songs, usually accompanied by guitar, beat-box, and sometimes the accordion, are mostly ballads of Haitian, Caribbean, or French origin.

Since the mid-1950s, the most popular commercial music in Haiti has been compas (*konpa* in Creole), a dance music that is a variant of a type of merengue played in the Dominican Republic but that also has roots in Central African soukous and North American jazz. For many years, the genre was dominated by the fierce competition between rival band leaders, Nemours Jean-Baptiste and Webert Sicot. Their battle for ascendancy became something of a national obsession, particularly at Carnival time. Compas grew in popularity across the country thanks to the advent of new radio stations that played popular music, and the development of a small black middle class who packed out the bands' concerts. Nowadays, the

New York-based Tabou Combo and the Miami-based T-Vice are two of the most popular Compas bands both in Haiti and among the Haitian diaspora.

Sweet Micky: Contemporary Compas

One of the most popular performers on the Haitian music scene over the last decade has been Michel Martelly, a.k.a Sweet Micky, a singer and keyboard player who plays a wild and raucous compas dance music. Sweet Micky's performances and recordings have given a new lease of life to a compas music scene that was becoming staid and conservative. Young Haitians are drawn not only to his infectious brand of dance music, but also to his non-conformist style and outrageous stage presence.

Born in 1961, Martelly grew up in the Port-au-Prince suburb of Carrefour, and released his first album, *Ou la la*, in 1989. His popularity rapidly increased as he cultivated an image as a hedonistic playboy, and touched a sympathetic nerve among those seeking to escape from everyday hardships. He soon enjoyed a national notoriety thanks to performances marked by his liberal use of *betiz* – Creole for playful and satirical obscenities – that form part of a repartee with the audience delivered in a slang mixture of English, French, and Creole. He also became known for his association with the military leaders who launched the coup d'état in September 1991. Many progressives spurned him for his willingness to play at concerts organized by the military regime, but young Haitians were thrilled to experience a rare opportunity to see and hear some live music during the coup years.

In an often very conservative country, Martelly's predilection for appearing on stage wearing a skirt, or even performing in full drag, as he did for the 1996 Carnival, is refreshingly daring. The incident at that Carnival involving the newly inaugurated President René Préval, is an example of Sweet Micky's popular bravado. Préval was watching the bands playing on the back of floats as they drove past the National Palace stage at the height of the Carnival. As the Sweet Micky float passed the VIP's stand, Martelly yelled, "President, I want to see you dancing. I don't want to see you dancing with your girlfriend; this would be too easy. I want you to get somebody from the crowd." Then he shouted, "Wait, wait, wait. I'm going to choose her," and he instructed someone to go up to the stand. The irreverent Martelly ordered Préval, "Now wait for me. When I tell you to move to the right, you move to the right." The crowd went crazy as Préval and his partner obeyed his instructions, shaking their hips right and then left, and thrusting back and forward.

In something of a reaction to Compas' Dominican origins and its association with the era of the Duvalier dictatorships, a new type of music influenced by *rara* and Vodou drumming developed in the 1980s. The roots, or *rasin*, music scene initially revolved around a few middle class Haitian kids, who were fed up with compas' party-time lyrics, and looked instead for inspiration to Bob Marley, reggae, and Rastafarianism in neighboring Jamaica. They got into Vodou, and especially into the Vodou drumming that was based on rhythms more or less unchanged since the time of slavery. On this percussive base, *rasin* groups such as Foula, Boukan Ginen, Kanpech, RAM, Koudyay, and Boukman Eksperyans, laid Hendrix and Santana-style guitar, and call and response vocals. Coinciding with the grassroots movement against dictatorship and the mobilization of the previously marginalized peasant majority, the *rasin* groups quickly captured the mood of the nation with lyrics that both criticized the military and praised Haitian peasant culture and beliefs.

Although Haiti appears to be the least Americanized of the Caribbean island cultures, the presence in the US and Canada of as many as two million Haitian-Americans and Haitian-Canadians – many of them now second and third generation – makes for an increasingly evident cultural crossover. Tens of thousands of Haitian-Americans come back to visit Haiti each year, especially at Carnival time and for the summer, and they bring with them the latest in US sounds and fashion. With the proliferation of radio stations playing US pop and soul music, it is not surprising that many young Haitians are now increasingly drawn to African-American hip-hop and rap styles that are popular in the United States. A new wave of rap bands in Haiti received a boost when the

Boukman Eksperyans   *Leah Gordon*

Carnival in Jacmel   *Leah Gordon*

Haitian-American rappers, the Fugees, played for free in front of over 80,000 people in downtown Port-au-Prince in early 1997. Following the Fugees' homecoming (Wyclef Jean and Pras Michel had left Haiti for the States when children), and especially when Jean released his solo album, *The Carnival*, featuring four songs sung in Creole, the genre took on a new cool with the slum kids of Port-au-Prince. As a result, a host of Creole-language rappers have become the new darlings of the Haitian music scene. Two of the most successful of these homemade Haitian rap groups are Original Rap Staff, and King Posse.

The changing nature of Haitian culture is also apparent in the evolution of Carnival in Haiti. This annual event takes place on the days before Ash Wednesday, climaxing on Mardi Gras night. Smaller versions take place in Cap-Haïtien and Les Cayes, but the main event is the Port-au-Prince Carnival where millions of revelers throng the streets around the central Champ de Mars area. The Port-au-Prince Carnival is a wild and boisterous affair that revolves around the procession of flatbed trucks on which Haitian dance bands play. The bands' floats usually set off around midnight, and begin a slow circuit, passing in front of spectators seated in specially erected stands that are sponsored by the producers of commercial products. Throughout the night the bands play their hits surrounded by huge dancing crowds. By contrast, the more traditional Jacmel Carnival, on the two Sundays before

Lent begins, is not only much more laid-back but is also a showcase for forms of creative expression other than dancing to amplified music. The Jacmel townspeople create spectacularly colorful papier-maché masks, and dress up as a host of weird creatures and characters. During the day, the Carnival performers take to the streets to enact a series of intriguing, and to the foreigner, quite obscure, vignettes and role-plays.

Literature

The golden age of Haitian literature was the 1930s and 1940s, when intellectuals wrestled with the concepts of black nationalism and cultural authenticity, and were influenced by ideas such as surrealism and Marxism. Some of the best writers were Carl Brouard, Jean Briere, Philippe-Thoby Marcelin, and Jacques Roumain. The latter founded the Haitian Communist Party in 1934, but his greatest legacy was his novel, *Masters of the Dew*, published posthumously in 1945. This influential book concerns a young man's efforts to save a once-thriving community from twin evils of drought and family feuds.

The latter part of the era produced two other great novelists whose work has since been translated into English. René Depestre's *Festival of the Greasy Pole* is a passionate insight into everyday life in Haiti during the repressive Duvalier era. Jacques Stéphen Alexis' masterpiece, *General Sun, My Brother*, reveals the suffering of Haitian peasant workers, and is rich with the details of peasant culture and myth. The advent of the Duvalier dictatorship forced most of the great Haitian writers into exile. Alexis was killed, presumably by the Tontons Macoutes, when he returned to Haiti in 1961.

More recently, a new generation of Haitian-American writers have been published to some acclaim. Two of the best known are the Montreal-based Dany Laferrière, and New York's Edwidge Danticat. The latter's *Breath, Eyes, Memory* (1994) became a bestseller when it was recommended on US national television by Oprah Winfrey.

People's Poet: Félix Morisseau-Leroy

The poet and playwright Félix Morisseau-Leroy pioneered, and to an extent legitimized, the use of the Creole language in literature and the performing arts. His seminal work was the Creole language version of Sophocles' *Antigone*, which was first performed in 1953 in Port-au-Prince. Until then, writers and intellectuals had always used French, and the staging of *Antigone* was the first time that Haitians could see a play performed in their own language.

He fled Haiti in 1959, when it became clear the dictator, François Duvalier, considered his work to be subversive, but continued to write and publish poems in Creole from exile in Senegal, and later in Miami, Florida. His work gave generations of Haitians a sense of pride in their native language.

In Morisseau-Leroy's poem, 'Sometimes I'm Not Myself ' (translated from Creole below), the influence of the spirits (*Iwa*) of the Vodou pantheon can be revolutionary:

Sometimes I'm not myself
There's a wild Iwa dancing in my head
A sorrowful Iwa that stamps on the ground
When it's like that I'm not myself
There's a huge drum beating in my heart
A marvelous Vodou is dancing in my body
When it's like that I can't say "darling"
It's comrade-friend I call you
If you take hold of my hand
There's a Iwa of revolution that's boiling in my blood
My horse is saddled
I'm set to go
A lambi of revolution is sounding
If you've the courage take my hand
My horse is saddled
Let's go.

Sport

Although there are signs that basketball is catching on, football (the US soccer) is by far the most popular sport in Haiti. Even in the countryside it is common to see flat areas with goal posts at either end – fields that double up for cattle-grazing and for use by the local soccer team. Despite the lack of decent playing fields, and the often prohibitive cost of team uniforms and balls, the game is immensely popular. In 1994, the right-wing newspaper, *Haiti Observateur*, in all seriousness attempted to rouse anti-intervention sentiment by suggesting that US troops were cordoning off soccer fields not just to use as helicopter landing sites but were also planning to convert them into baseball parks.

The country's finest hour as a footballing nation was in 1974 when, thanks in no small part to the patronage of Jean-Claude Duvalier, the national side succeeded in qualifying for the World Cup final – the first Caribbean nation to do so. Haiti's appearances in the matches in West Germany were not successful, although the team did briefly hold a lead over Italy. With the political upheavals that followed in the 1980s and 90s, the game experienced a decline at a national level. Recently though, there has been something of a renaissance with the French-funded renovation of the national stadium in the capital, the appointment of Manno Sanon – hero of the 1974 team – as a national team coach, and the development of training facilities at what was once the Duvaliers' holiday ranch at Croix-des-Bouquets.

At a local level, the game is well-organized, with hundreds of small clubs competing for both men and women's leagues. One of the most inspiring development projects in the country is the new soccer club, Athletic d'Haiti, based at Drouillard, not far from the notorious slum of Cité Soleil. Wasteland has been flattened and cleared for soccer fields, and ruined buildings have been renovated to serve as changing rooms and a club house. Volunteers organize games for the local children and teenagers who are given a rare opportunity to hone their skills.

WHERE TO GO, WHAT TO SEE

Millions of tourists visit the Caribbean for their holidays, and some of Haiti's neighbors, like Jamaica, Cuba, and the Dominican Republic, are now the biggest destinations. Few people, however, visit Haiti, and it is easy to see why. Since the Club Med closed its doors, there are no all-inclusive resorts of the sort that have made the Dominican Republic so popular. Visitors must make their own way to a hotel, and in most cases will need to hire a car to explore. Throughout the country, roads are appalling, the electricity supply sporadic, and the vast majority live in dire poverty. Hurricanes, insurrections, and termites mean that few examples of colonial architecture remain. If you are looking for a relaxing vacation with European standard facilities and communications it's advisable to go elsewhere.

On the other hand, Haiti's spectacular mountains and undeveloped coastline, the people's social and cultural links with their West African ancestry, and their vibrant Vodou religion and associated artistic creativity, make it well worth a visit. In a world where one country is starting to look much like another, Haiti is still startlingly fresh to the jaded Western traveler. If you have a spirit of adventure and can take the rough with the smooth, Haiti can be an awe-inspiring and memorable experience.

The capital, Port-au-Prince, can be a daunting place for the newly-arrived, who will be greeted by a mass of pedestrians, ramshackle vehicles invariably blocked and pot-holed roads, and disorganized street markets set amidst open drains and burning piles of trash greets you. There is a order of sorts in this apparent chaos, and it is worth braving the streets on foot in order to get a sense of what city life is all about. Here, as in the rest of the country, it is the people and their way of life that are the main attraction.

Visitors might want to orient themselves by locating the central Champs de Mars, a series of small parks crisscrossed by roads that link the commercial center with the residential areas built on the hillsides leading up to the suburb of Pétionville. The recently renovated Champs de Mars area is dominated by the Presidential Palace, built in 1918 during the US occupation, and clearly modeled on the Washington White House. Opposite the palace are two monuments to Haiti's historic struggle for liberty. The Marron Inconnu (Unknown Slave) is a runaway slave warrior carrying a machete and blowing through a conch shell to call for assistance. Next to it is the Martyrs' Square, and its centerpiece, a statue commemorating the victims of the recent military regimes.

Labadie beach

Leah Gordon

Other nearby places of interest are the small National Museum, the Museum of Haitian Art, and the St. Trinité Episcopal Cathedral, famed for its murals by some of the great Haitian painters.

The downtown area toward the seafront has little to recommend it, although a visit to the Iron Market is worthwhile. Further south, near where the endless suburb of Carrefour begins, is the National Cemetery, a vast expanse of tombs and sepulchral sculptures. It is worth a look, and is a must on November 1st and 2nd when celebrants honor the Gede spirit family in an annual Vodou festival. Up the hill from the cemetery is the Oloffson Hotel, a Haitian institution, and without doubt one of the most atmospheric hotels in the world. The setting for much of Graham Greene's 1964 novel, *The Comedians*, the hotel is all creaking wooden floors, ornate latticework, and cool verandas overlooking an oasis-like garden, and this just a stone's throw from the throbbing chaos of downtown Port-au-Prince. Today the Greene connection brings in a few guests who, together with a steady trickle of foreign correspondents, aid workers, and danger-seekers, just about keep the hotel going. The Vodou rock band RAM plays in the lounge most Thursday nights.

Most other hotels are to be found in Pétionville, four miles up the hill. It's the home of Haiti's elite families, and as such is quite unlike anywhere else in the country. Here you'll find top quality French cuisine, Internet cafes, casinos, and nightclubs. Rasin and Konpa bands usually play on

Friday and Saturday nights, and boards advertising the performances are put up at strategic road junctions. A few miles further up the mountainside, at Fermathe, are the ruins of Fort Jacques, built by Jean-Jacques Dessalines in expectation of a French invasion. Higher up still is the village of Kenscoff, where the surrounding countryside is a great place to breathe fresh air, admire fabulous views, and unwind from the rigors of the city.

Moving away from the capital to the south, the road follows the coast along the Léogâne plain. The first main road to the south takes the traveler up and over a stunning mountain range. It leads to the coastal town of Jacmel, an essential destination for any visitor. Once a thriving coffee port, it is now a picturesque haven of tranquillity where there is not much to do but wander around the nearly empty streets admiring the wrought-iron balconies of the nineteenth century New Orleans-style mansions. One of the finest buildings is the Manoir Alexandra Hotel, which overlooks the town square to one side and the magnificent bay of Jacmel to the other. Jacmel's residents still practice Carnival arts in the traditional way, and even if you can't make it for the annual pre-Lenten display of costumes and masks, at any time of the year you should look out for the craftsmen's huts along the seafront lane.

North from Port-au-Prince the road again hugs the coast, passing through fields of banana and plantain trees. Dotted along this stretch of the coast are many beach clubs, where for the admission price of few dollars you can sip rum punch while lying on a sun bed. The Cotes des Arcadins beaches are the best ones within a few hours drive from Port-au-Prince, and are well-frequented at weekends. Beyond the small port town of St. Marc the road turns inland and crosses the rice fields of the vast Artibonite plain. With a four wheel drive, it's possible to turn off at Pont Sondé, and travel up the almost totally unspoiled Artibonite river valley until you reach the third of Haiti's three main roads at Mirebalais. From there, the intrepid traveler can head north into the remote and beautiful Central Plateau, or take the incredibly rough route south back to Port-au-Prince.

Continuing on the main road north across the Artibonite plain, the road eventually rises up through mountains and winds its way to the former capital, Cap-Haïtien. Le Cap, as it is known, is a relaxed city with narrow streets laid out in a geometric grid. The town houses are built close together and so provide welcome shade from the fierce sun. Le Cap offers little excitement itself but is a good base from which to explore the beaches and historic monuments in the surrounding area. Some of the best beaches in all Haiti are to be found to the west of the city, five miles along a rough road. Cormier Plage is a superior beach resort and restaurant, but beyond it are the more spectacular beaches of the Labadie peninsula. Make sure to visit on a day when the cruise ship is not stopping, unless you want to share the sand with several hundred others.

Sans Souci Palace, Milot

Leah Gordon

In the other direction, east from Cap-Haïtien, near the town of Milot, are the ruins of the once fabulous Sans Souci Palace. Built by King Henri Christophe in the early decades of the nineteenth century as the Caribbean counterpart to Frederick the Great's Potsdam Palace, Sans Souci was partly destroyed by earthquake in 1842. It is still a pleasant and peaceful place to visit and daydream about Haiti's incredible history. Rising above Sans Souci is the massive La Ferrièrre mountain upon which is perched the Citadelle, one of the most spectacular constructions in the Caribbean. Christophe's staggeringly impressive fortress is 3,000 feet above sea level, and boasts 12-foot thick walls and 140-foot high ramparts. Connoisseurs of military ruins might want to visit the town of Fort Liberté, near to the border with the Dominican Republic, where Fort Dauphin, built by the French in 1730, is the best preserved part of a complex of fortifications.

The really adventurous traveler could make the arduous trip, via Gonaïves, to the northwestern town of Port-de-Paix, and from there cross by boat to the remote island of La Tortue. On the furthermost western end of the island, at the appropriately named Pointe Oueste, is what some visitors have described as the best beach in the whole Caribbean. La Tortue Island truly is the back of beyond, and only the most determined of hikers should consider going.

TIPS FOR TRAVELERS

When to Go

Haiti is hot all year, but it is slightly cooler, and therefore better for travelling in the winter months, whereas the summer months can be so unbearably hot that at times it is almost impossible to stand in the full sun. In the mountains at night it can get quite cold, but this should not be a major concern as nearly all accommodations are located in lowland areas. Dusty streets and muddy tracks, and high humidity mean it's a good idea to bring plenty of light, easily cleaned clothes. The timing of the country's rainy seasons is a constant source of speculation among Haiti's peasant farmers, but nowadays it is increasingly a question of whether the rain that does fall will be sufficient to seep into the topsoil. Rainy seasons have traditionally occurred in late spring and fall, but such has been the extent of deforestation that the climate pattern is now undergoing significant, and for the farmers, potentially catastrophic changes.

The hurricane season is still a reliable fixture, and torrential rain and strong winds are liable to sweep across the country at any time between September and November. High season fares (summer and New Year) for transatlantic routes can be as much as double those at other times of the year.

Getting Around

In Port-au-Prince it's possible to get around and see most things using public transportation. The brightly-painted minibuses and pickups, known as *tap-taps*, connect most parts of the city, while the shared taxis – identified by a red ribbon hanging from the rear view mirror – will take you to a specific destination but only if it is to the driver's liking. Both modes of transportation are cheap, and making the effort to use them is recommended as one of the best ways to get a taste of everyday life. On the other hand, if you don't have the time to get confused, disorientated, or stuck in unending traffic jams, you should consider hiring a guide with a car, but you must be prepared for some hard bargaining to arrive at a decent price. Another option is to rent your own car, either from the agencies at the airport, or telephone the company and ask them to bring the car to your hotel. However you should be warned that driving the streets of Port-au-Prince requires great determination and concentration.

Outside the capital, your own car is more or less a must, and unless you are planning to stick to the roads to Cap-Haïtien, Jacmel or Les Cayes, a four-wheel drive is an absolute necessity. All other roads (perhaps more accurately described as tracks) are in quite deplorable condition. Remember to drive with consideration for the pedestrians and animals that use the roads too, and watch out for kamikaze bus drivers. To get a sense of the reality of Haitian life, be sure stop along the route, and get out of your car as much as possible. For those making just a short visit but wanting to explore further afield, it is worth considering the local airline, Caribintair, that flies daily to both Cap-Haïtien, and to the remote and little-visited southern town of Jérémie.

Money

The only foreign currency that means anything in Haiti is the US dollar, and it is possible to change this into the local currency, the gourde, in hotels, banks, and even on the street. Changing money at a bank is the best option, as there you will usually find a better rate of exchange, and, unlike when using the street money-changers, are likely to be given the correct amount of gourdes. The larger banks will also pay out cash against a major credit card. A major source of confusion for newcomers to Haiti is the persistent use of the term "Haitian dollar" when no such unit of currency physically exists. This anomaly is a legacy of the time long ago when the local currency was pegged to the US dollar at the rate of five Haitian gourdes to one US dollar. Ever since, five Haitian gourdes have been known as one Haitian dollar. To avoid misunderstandings when bartering for a service or agreeing to a transaction, clarify whether the price is in gourdes, or Haitian or American dollars.

Security

It is a sad fact that common crime is on the increase in Haiti. Once more or less socially taboo, petty theft and burglary are now increasingly common ways to try to escape from crushing poverty. Foreigners are not usually specific targets, and visitors to Haiti should take the normal precautions. Don't show off valuable jewelry or video cameras, or carry large amounts of cash. If mugged, it is advisable to hand over what is demanded. Theft from cars is on the increase, and nothing should be left on view in an unattended vehicle. At any time local people may erect barricades across the road to halt the traffic in order to draw attention to what are usually genuine grievances. Visitors should not attempt to cross these roadblocks. Although the hold-up may be inconvenient, it is better to admire the Haitian peoples' spirit than to get wound up. The increase in common crime, and the very recent and ongoing experiences of political violence, make most Haitians reluctant to travel after dark, and newly-arrived tourists should probably not stay out too late at night either.

Health

All visitors must be covered by travel insurance because only the handful of private hospitals can offer any kind of adequate service in the unfortunate event of accident or serious illness. Polio, tetanus, diphtheria, typhoid, hepatitis A, rabies, and malaria are all potential risks, and visitors should seek medical advice on preventative treatment and inoculations well in advance of arrival in Haiti. Mosquito bites are a major irritation, as well as carrying the risk of malaria. A mosquito net, and ample supplies of insect repellent and bite soothing cream are recommended. Always use bottled water, even for brushing teeth – the locally produced Culligan brand water is fine. HIV/AIDS is a serious problem – a local brand of condoms, called *Pantè*, can be purchased from street traders nearly everywhere.

FURTHER READING AND BOOKSTORES

Fact:

Arthur, C. & Dash, M., eds. *Libète: A Haiti Anthology*. London, 1999.

Averill, G.A. *Day for the Hunter, a Day for the Prey: Popular Music and Power in Haiti*. Chicago, 1997.

Cadet, J-R. *Restavec: From Haitian Slave Child to Middle Class American*. Texas, 1998.

Courlander, H. *The Drum and the Hoe*. Berkeley, 1960.

Deren, M. *Divine Horsemen: The Living Gods of Haiti*. 1953.

Ferguson, J. *Papa Doc, Baby Doc: Haiti and the Duvaliers*. Oxford, 1988.

Fick, C. *The Making of Haiti: the Saint Domingue Revolution from Below*. Knoxville, 1990.

Gordon, L. and Doggett, S. *The Lonely Planet Guide to Haiti and the Dominican Republic*. Victoria, 1999

Gordon, L. *The Book of Vodou*. London, 2000.

Hurbon, L. *Voodoo: Truth and Fantasy/Search for the Spirit.** London, 1995.

James, C.L.R. *The Black Jacobins*. London, 1938.

NACLA, ed. *Haiti: Dangerous Crossroads*. Denver, 1995.

McGowan, L./Development Gap. *Democracy Undermined, Economic Justice Denied*. 1997.

Richardson, L./Grassroots International. *Feeding Dependency, Starving Democracy: USAID Policies in Haiti*. 1997.

Thomson, I. *Bonjour Blanc: A Journey through Haiti*. London, 1993.

Trouillot, M-R. *Haiti: State against Nation*. New York, 1990.

Wilentz, A. *The Rainy Season: Haiti since the Duvaliers*. London, 1994.

Fiction:

Alexis, Jacques Stéphen. *General Sun, My Brother*. Charlottesville, 1999.

Banks, Russell. *Continental Drift*. New York, 1985.

Carpentier, Alejo. *The Kingdom of this World*. London, 1957.

Danticat, Edwidge. *Krik? Krak!*. 1994.

Danticat, Edwidge, ed. *The Butterfly's Way: Voices from the Haitian Diaspora in the United States*. 2001

Dépestre, René. *Festival of the Greasy Pole*. Charlottesville, 1990.

Greene, Graham. *The Comedians*. London, 1967.

Metéllus, Jean. *The Vortex Family*. London, 1995.

Montera, M. *You, Darkness/In the Palm of Darkness.** 1998.

Morisseau-Leroy, Félix. *Haitiad & Oddities*. Miami, 1991.

Roumain, Jacques. *Masters of the Dew*. London, 1978.

(* US title)

Recommended Listening:

> *Angels in the Mirror: Vodou Music of Haiti* – various
> *Caribbean Revels: Haitian Rara and Dominican Gaga* – various
> *Haiti Cheri* – various
> *Maximum Compas* – Coupé Cloué
> *Best of Michel Marthelly* – Sweet Mickey
> *Respect* – Tabou Combo
> *Banm T-Vice Mwen* – T-Vice
> *Kalfou Danjerè* – Boukman Eksperyans
> *Revolution* – Boukman Eksperyans
> *Jou a Rive* – Boukan Ginen
> *Puritan Vodou* – RAM
> *Si* – Beethova Obas
> *Tout Mon Temps* – Emeline Michel
> *Carnival* – Wyclef Jean and the Refugee All Stars

Recommended Surfing:

> Windows on Haiti – www.windowsonhaiti.com – a wide-ranging site with photos, commentaries, music reviews, book recommendations, and links.
> Bob Corbett's Haiti Page – www.webster.edu/~corbetre/haiti/haiti.html – a huge collection of texts dealing with history and culture.
> The Haiti Support Group – www.gn.apc.org/haitisupport – site of the British solidarity organization.
> The Quixote Center – www.quixote.org/haiti/ – site of the US solidarity organization.

Local Bookstores

> Librarie La Pleiade
> 83 rue des Miracles
> Port-au-Prince
>
> La Pleiade
> La Promenade
> Pétionville
>
> Panoramix
> Rue A (rue 11/12)
> Cap-Haïtien

ADDRESSES AND CONTACTS

DOA/BN - Haiti Travels
PO Box 15451
Pétionville
Haiti
(509) 246-0477 and (509) 401-2634 (messages only)
e-mail: crb@maf.org
website: www.haititravels.com

Voyages Lumière - Journeys for the enlightened traveler
Pétionville
Haiti
e-mail: ljacqui@haitiworld.com

Global Exchange - Reality Tours
2017 Mission Street #303
San Francisco, CA 94110
(415) 255-7296
e-mail: moira@globalexchange.org
website: www.globalexchange.org/tours

Kiskeya Alternative Destination - Eco and alternative tourism in Haiti
and the Dominican Republic
P.O.Box 109-Z
Zona Colonial
Santo Domingo
Dominican Republic
(809) 537 89 77
e-mail: kad@kiskeya-alternative.org
website: www.kiskeya-alternative.org

Embassy of the Republic of Haiti
2311 Massachusetts Avenue, N.W.
Washington, DC 20008
(202) 332 4090
e-mail: embassy@haiti.org
website: www.haiti.org

FACTS AND FIGURES

Official name: République d'Haïti.

Situation: The western third of the island of Hispaniola, bordering the Dominican Republic, between 17 and 20 N, and 68 and 75 W.

Surface area: 10,700 sq. mi. (27,750 km²)

Climate: Tropical with average daily temperatures ranging from 23 to 34C (73 to 93F) in the hottest month, July, and from 20 to 31C (68 to 88F) in the coldest month, January. The amount of rain varies greatly between different regions, with about 16 in. (40cm) of rain each year in the arid northwest, and 160 in. (400cm) of rain a year in the highest mountains. In general, the higher the elevation, the cooler and wetter it gets. As a consequence of the severe deforestation of the country, the rainy seasons are now no longer as regular as they used to be, but prolonged showers are most likely around April and May. The island of Hispaniola lies in the middle of the hurricane belt, and violent storms, gales, and torrential rainfall can be expected during the hurricane season from September through November. In November 1994 Hurricane Gordon left a trail of death and destruction across the south of Haiti, and in September 1998 Hurricane George brought floods and mudslides to the center, causing over 250 deaths and making thousands homeless.

Relief and landscape: Three-quarters of Haiti is mountainous terrain. The northern and southern peninsulas are dominated by vast mountain ranges. The highest point is the Pic La Selle (8,744 ft./2,674 m), southeast of Port-au-Prince, closely followed by Pic Macaya (7,675 ft./ 2,347m), south of Jérémie. In the center, the Montagnes Noires and the Chaine des Matheux stand either side of Haiti's one great river, the Artibonite, which flows for 174 miles (280 km) down a long valley before eventually crossing the wide and flat Artibonite Plain. Other lowland areas are the Central Plateau, and the numerous plains, the most notable of which are the Plaine du Nord, south and east of Cap-Haïtien, the Plaine des Cayes in the south, and the Plaine du Cul de Sac and Plaine de Léogâne, respectively stretching east and west of Port-au-Prince. The largest lake is the salt-water Etang Saumatre that forms a natural boundary between the Plaine du Cul de Sac and the Dominican Republic. Péligre Lake was formed in the early 1950s when the upper Artibonite River was dammed to generate hydro-electric power. The four main islands are La Gonâve, in the gulf between the two peninsulas; La Tortue, off the north coast; and the much smaller Ile-à-Vache and Grande Cayemite in the south.

Flora and fauna: There is an immense variety of flora, with an estimated 5,000 species of flowering plants and conifers, a third of them endemic, and over 600 species of orchids. By far the greatest variety of flora is found in the areas of heaviest rainfall, the highest mountain ranges. There are also 220 species of birds, 21 of them endemic, and two endemic mammals – the rodent, zagouti (Plagiodontia), and the insectivore, longue nez (Solenodon). Many of the endemic species are threatened with extinction as a consequence of extensive deforestation and the resulting erosion of topsoil. Forest cover has rapidly declined, from about 60 percent of the national area in 1923 to less than

2 percent by the late 1990s. In excess of 4 million cubic meters of wood (nearly all of it charcoal) are consumed each year to provide energy for cooking and dry cleaning. Approximately a third of the country is severely eroded. Four national parks have been created to try to preserve some of Haiti's forests, and, in so doing, protect some of the country's remaining watersheds: the largest is the Forêt des Pins (Pine Forest) in the southeast; much smaller are the tropical, cloud forest reserves at Pic Macaya, south of Jérémie, and Parc La Visite, south of Port-au-Prince. The region around the Citadelle La Ferrière, south of Cap-Haïtien, was recognized by UNESCO as a National Historic Park in 1982.
Infrastructure: Road conditions remain very poor despite recent rehabilitation projects funded by international donors, particularly the European Union. It was estimated in 1996 that out of a total 2,579 miles (4,160 km) of roads in Haiti, only about a quarter were paved. Even those stretches that are paved are generally potholed and unreliable. There are really only two main roads, one that runs north from Port-au-Prince to Cap-Haïtien, and the other southwest from Port-au-Prince to Les Cayes. Apart from these two roads, and the road over the mountains from Carrefour Dufort to Jacmel, and the road from the capital to the Malpasse border crossing, other routes cannot usually be traveled by car, and require transportation by jeep or truck. A railway once ran from Léogâne to Port-au-Prince, and then north along the coast via St Marc, before turning inland and along the Artibonite Valley, but the tracks were pulled up and sold off during the Duvalier era. Narrow-gauge railway lines that used to transport sugar cane in lowland areas fell into disrepair when the last three large-scale sugar refineries closed down in 1986. There is one international airport at Port-au-Prince served by American Airlines, Air Canada, Air France, ALM, and Copa, and an ever-changing roster of small local airlines. From the short airstrip at Cap-Haïtien it is possible to take a small plane for flights to Fort Lauderdale in the US, and to Providenciales in the British Turks and Caicos Islands. The local carrier, Caribintair, flies small planes between Port-au-Prince and Santo Domingo, and provides the only internal service, linking the capital with Cap-Haïtien and Jérémie. Port-au-Prince is the major port with container facilities. Miragoâne is the main port for exports, while Cap-Haïtien is the country's third significant port.
Administrative divisions: 9 departments, divided into 135 municipalities and 565 communal sections.
Capital: Port-au-Prince, population 2 million (2004 estimate).
Other large towns (population estimates 1997): Cap-Haïtien (80,000), Les Cayes (50,000), Gonaïves (50,000), Jacmel (15,000).

POPULATION

(2004 estimates)
Population: 7.66 million (1990: 6.5 million).
Ethnic composition: 95% black, 5% mulatto and white.
Population growth rate: 1.71%.
Urban population: 37.5%.
Rural population: 62.5%.
Population density: 719 per square mile; 278 per square km.
Birth rate: 33.76 per 1,000.
Death rate: 13.21 per 1,000.
Population by age: 0–14 years, 42.2%; 15–64 years, 54.1%; 65+ years, 3.7%.
Children per woman: A

Progressistes (Assembly of Progressive National Democrats), PANPRA – Parti Nationaliste Progressiste Revolutionnaire Haitien (Haitian Revolutionary Progressive Nationalist Party), KONAKOM – Komite Nasyonal Kongres Oganizasyons Demokratik (National Congress of Democratic Movements), MDN – Mobilization pour le Développement National (Mobilization for National Development).

Membership of international organizations: United Nations and UN organizations; Organization of American States; African, Caribbean and Pacific group linked to the European Union; Caribbean economic community – CARICOM (provisional membership).

HAITI AND THE US/EU

Since the US occupation of 1915–1994, the Haitian economy has been linked to its powerful northern neighbor. The traditional exports, coffee and sugar, were sent north, as were sisal, during the Second World War, and bauxite, in the post-war period. During the 1970s, the manufacturing assembly sector took off – US companies provided Haitian sub-contractors with US-sourced materials to produce sporting goods, clothing, and basic electrical units, to be sold to the US market. Haiti joined the Lomé Convention with the European Union (EU) in 1989, and Italy and France have grown in importance as export customers for coffee. The US has also been the main source of imports, particularly food and luxury goods, although large-scale smuggling makes a complete picture hard to compile. The reduction and eventual elimination of import tariffs in the late 1990s has opened Haiti to even greater amounts of foreign goods, particularly rice and meat from the US and consumer items from the Dominican Republic. Haiti has long been dependent on international aid. Millions of dollars in aid were provided by international financial institutions during the 1970s and 1980s but to little effect – much of the aid was stolen by the Jean-Claude Duvalier regime. In the aftermath of the 1991–1994 military coup period, international aid was resumed on a large scale. The International Monetary Fund, the World Bank, the Inter-American Development Bank, and the European Union put together an aid package amounting to US$2.5 billion over 5 years. Most of this aid was offered on low, and long-term, interest repayment terms, although the European Union aid is almost entirely in the form of donations. The US, through its Agency for International Development, has been by far the most important bilateral donor. In the late 1990s, the British Department for International Development began a modest aid program for Haiti, but Anglo-Haitian relations remain very low-key. The British ambassador was expelled from Haiti by François Duvalier in 1962, and direct diplomatic relations were never renewed. A small step forward was made with the 1998 transfer of responsibility for Haiti from the British Embassy in Kingston, Jamaica, to the closer one in Santo Domingo, the Dominican Republic.